D0182761

THE
SOCIOLOGY
OF
HEALTH
AND
MEDICINE

Nicky Hart

P45
79

MERTHYR TYDFIL COLLEGE
LIBRARY

Causeway Books

S. 1. 306.46
ACC 7073

Nicky Hart is a lecturer in sociology at the University of Essex and acted as research fellow to the DHSS Inequalities in Health Working Group whose report is known as the 'Black Report'.

British Library Cataloguing in Publication Data

Hart, Nicky
  The sociology of health and medicine.—(Themes and
  perspectives in sociology)
  1. Social medicine
  I. Title II. Series
  306'.46   RA418

Causeway Press Ltd.
PO Box 13, Ormskirk, Lancashire L39 5HP
© Nicky Hart 1985

1st Impression June 1985
Reprinted 1985, 1988, 1991, 1992, 1993

Typesetting by Lloyd Williams, Southport
Printed and bound by The Alden Press, Oxford

Contents

Chapter Five
Becoming Ill as a Social Process

Chapter Six
Medicine as an Institution of Social Control

Chapter Seven
The Power of Medicine in Society

Bibliography 133

Index 135

Chapter One

Health and the Mythology of Medicine

The Relationship between Health and Medicine

In present day Britain, it is difficult for most people to separate their ideas about health from their ideas about medicine. This is because the medical profession has successfully persuaded us that our personal health depends upon high standards of medical care. As a result, the National Health Service (NHS), has been designed as a national medical service. It consists almost entirely of surgeries, clinics and hospitals and it is the mainstay of government policy for health. In maintaining it as a system of free medical advice and almost free treatment, at an annual cost of more than 5% of national income (£15 billion in 1982), the government reckons that it has discharged its duty to protect the nation's health. In fact so complete is the grip of the medical profession over both popular and political consciousness that to most people medicine is synonymous with health.

What's wrong with this state of affairs? Surely the medical profession has every right to monopolise national health policy? Have they not earned it through the demonstrable effectiveness of their knowledge and skill? Surprisingly, the answers to these questions are all in the negative. Medicine has not made a significant contribution to improving people's health in the past and much of the treatment carried out in the NHS today has never been carefully evaluated. Obviously some forms of medical intervention are highly successful. But because they cannot be separated from unsuccessful techniques, we cannot measure the contribution of medicine to contemporary levels of health. An example may help to clarify this point. Every year in Britain, thousands of people suffering from lung cancer are treated in the NHS. The consultants responsible for them are well aware that probably less than 5% will derive any benefit from the treatment which for the majority might even be worse than the effects of the disease itself in what is likely to be the final year of the person's life. This is why some people reject the offer of medical help. But because treatment is not evaluated, we do not know how many people survive and for how long. Some routine treatment, e.g. the repair of fractures, is self-evidently beneficial. But in the absence of statistical records of the outcome of all treatment, we have no way of knowing the value of resources expended in the NHS, both in the financial sense and in terms of their contribution to the nation's health. The remainder of this chapter will be devoted to proving the truth of these statements. But before going on to examine the evidence, we should clarify what we mean by *health.*

The Concept of Health

The concept of health is difficult to define and measure. Although we associate it with the activities of doctors, it is only indirectly linked to medical treatment. Doctors deal primarily with disease and not with the promotion of health in any positive way. The knowledge of medicine is a catalogue of disorders implying that when none are present people are healthy. But to promote health involves the prevention of disease, not merely its treatment. Given that limited scope exists to restore or repair damaged health (see pp.7-9), there is little to be learned about health as such in medical literature.

So what is health and what are the factors that protect it or put it at risk? At a personal level we all know the answer at least to the first of these questions. We know from personal experience of feeling well and feeling ill how to distinguish health and ill-health in subjective terms. But converting subjective knowledge into a standard measure which applies to the whole population is by no means easy. To begin with, not everybody has the same threshold of pain or the same expectations about what counts as abnormal symptoms. Some people go to the doctor for complaints which others may not even notice and yet the latter include people who spend a whole lifetime apparently feeling healthy only to die at an early age of a preventable or treatable condition. The problem is finding a definition for health which covers these variations and permits the measurement of health experience in the population as a whole.

The World Health Organisation (WHO) defines health as, 'Not merely the absence of disease and infirmity but complete physical, mental and social wellbeing'. (WHO, 1955). This definition emphasises the interdependence of physical and mental welfare, stressing that feeling well is not just a physical experience. But how can these different dimensions be converted into a measure which can be used to study the distribution of health in one society or to compare standards of health between societies? In the absence of any universally valid measure, most surveys of health rely on one or other of the health status indicators of *morbidity* and *mortality.*

The first of these, morbidity, which means quite simply sickness, is an indicator not of health but of its absence. It is measured either through self reported illness in health surveys or from the statistics of time off work. Alternatively it may be constructed from the records of consultation between doctors and patients. The statistics of morbidity in any of these forms represent health negatively as a state of illness at one point in time. As such they tend to convey the impression of ill-health in episodic terms as something that happens suddenly and then goes away, rather than as a continuous dimension of experience. They also pose a number of problems of interpretation when applied for the purposes of comparing health experience within a population. Self reported sickness has the shortcoming already mentioned of being based on subjective judgement. Thus statistics of sickness absence can only represent the experience of people at work, while those of medical treatment are as much a measure of availability of, as demand for, services. Given the substantial variation found all over Britain in the length of waiting lists for different kinds of treatment, records of medical consultation and treatment provide a limited picture of the extent of morbidity in the population, and an even more limited indicator of its health in any positive sense.

What of the other health status indicator, mortality? This measure of health is constructed from mortality statistics. It can provide information about the risk of death at any age and from any particular cause. Its great limitation is that it only represents forms of ill-health that are ultimately fatal and not all those other forms of pain and suffering that do not result in loss of life. However it is not influenced by the processes of subjective judgement in the way that morbidity is and, being a more objective measure, it can be used to study changes over time. In fact the incidence of mortality is the only means of studying health in earlier times before the introduction of the NHS, national insurance schemes and the questionnaire survey. Age at death provides a measure of the length of the human lifetime. It indicates, in other words, the durability of the human body, the time it takes to wear out. In this sense mortality is a particularly useful indicator. It captures the positive dimension of health and it avoids the trap of presenting ill-health as an episodic event.

Life expectation is the only means of making any sense of what people's health was like in the nineteenth century and before. In the remainder of this book, we shall make extensive use of this measure to study (1) the contribution of medicine to improvements in health in both the past and the present, (2) the impact of social and economic change on health in the nineteenth and twentieth centuries and (3) the extent of social inequality in health.

Health and Medicine: The Historical Balance Sheet

During the last 150 years the causes of death in Britain have been gradually transformed. Before 1900, infective diseases like tuberculosis accounted for most deaths at every age, yet today they have virtually disappeared. Their place has been taken by accidents among young people and by heart disease and cancer among middle-aged and older people. These changes are examined in more detail in chapter 2 (p.20). The elimination of fatal infections has been associated with a 'leap forward' in life expectation. People live longer today than they ever did in the past and the fact that human bodies have become more durable, is the most important evidence of better health in the modern world.

Table 1.1 gives changes in life expectation since 1830 and reveals the improvements that have taken place especially at birth.

Table 1.1   Expectation of Life at Selected Ages by Sex

Period	Birth		Age 15		Age 65	
	Male	Female	Male	Female	Male	Female
1838-1854	39.9	41.8	43.2	43.9	10.8	11.5
1891-1900	44.1	47.8	45.2	47.6	10.3	11.3
1950-1952	66.5	71.5	54.4	58.9	11.7	14.3
1974-1976	69.6	75.8	56.2	62.1	12.4	16.4

Source: *The Demographic Review* 1977 p.19 (England and Wales)

The increase in life expectation at birth from around 40 years in the first half of the nineteenth century to 70 and over in the mid 1970s, means that the majority of babies born today can expect to live to the age of 60 and beyond. During the same period, an increase of 13 and 18 years for males and females respectively at age 15 has been achieved.

When and why did the decline in mortality come about? Most observers agree with McKeown that the fall began around 1830. It was made up of a combination of causes but more than 60% of the total decline between 1850 and 1970 was due to a reduction in infective conditions. Among them, the most important single cause was tuberculosis or as it was popularly known in the last century, *consumption.* The decline of this disease is shown in Figure 1.1 From an annual level of more than 4000 per million population in the second half of the nineteenth century, the incidence of TB had fallen to less than 500 by the time that drugs became available for its treatment in 1947. As figure 1.1, demonstrates the bulk of the decline took place well before this time and the slope of the gradient is only slightly altered by the introduction of effective medical treatment. The reductio threat of TB in Britain must therefore have been stimulated by other than medical factors and there is no reason to suppose that these same factors did not continue to account for most of the further decline of the disease after the introduction of chemotherapy - in plain language, antibiotics.

Figure 1.1 Respiratory Tuberculosis: The Decline in England and Wales, 1840-1970

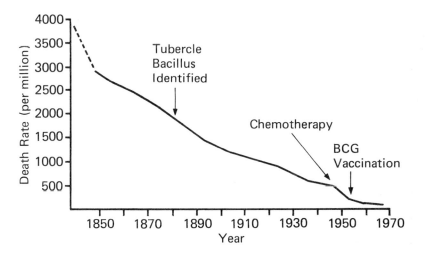

Source: McKeown, T., *The Modern Rise of Population,* Edward Arnold, London, 1976, p.81.

All of the other *major* diseases that declined, measles, scarlet fever, pneumonia, bronchitis and whooping cough, tell the same story - a steady decline beginning well before the introduction of effective treatment leaving only a relatively small residue of cases by the time vaccination or effective drugs become available. From then on it is difficult to separate the impact of medical treatment from the continuing influence of the factors which began the decline in the first place. It all suggests that the threat of infective micro-organisms (viruses) to human health was being systematically swept away not by improvements in medical science but by other events and processes which are new to the nineteenth and twentieth centuries.

It is important to recognise that the fall in the death rate that occurred in the last century was not merely the result of the disappearance of a series of different diseases, it was rather the disappearance of the whole class of disease that had afflicted human beings and curtailed the human lifespan from time immemorial. Improvements in life expectation are largely the product of this revolutionary change in human health and medicine played a very peripheral part in bringing them about. But what of the other causes of death that have declined - is the record of medical achievement any better there?

The eighteenth and nineteenth centuries saw a tremendous growth in the number of hospitals in London and the provinces. It was during this period that many of the famous teaching hospitals were established. On the face of it, this must surely have had some effect on the health of the population. But did it? It is difficult to find evidence to assess the effectiveness of hospital treatment on individual patients because few records were kept. This is also true for the present day; rates of survival following hospital treatment are not recorded by the NHS. But we can get some idea of the contribution of hospitals by estimating the adequacy of their methods of treatment in the light of present day knowledge. Proceeding in this way McKeown is led to the conclusion that hospitals could not have made an appreciable impact on the population's health before the twentieth century. Techniques of surgery were very primitive by modern standards and death rates from it were very high. Like heart transplants in the present day, surgical intervention, in the absence of anaesthesia and antiseptic methods, was a rather experimental affair and only attempted when the patient was likely to die anyway. At this time too, what Illich has called *iatrogenic* conditions (see p.46) i.e. sickness brought about by medical treatment itself, were widespread. In the lying-in hospitals (predecessors of today's maternity hospitals), maternal death rates from puerperal fever were much higher on wards where infants were delivered by doctors. Doctors ignorant of the risk of infection, examined patients with hands smothered with the debris of postmortem examinations. As McKeown concludes,

> . . . on balance the effects of hospital work in this period were probably harmful . . . any patient faced the risk of contracting a lethal infection up to the second half of the nineteenth century . . . and it was not until much later that hospital patients could be reasonably certain of dying from the diseases with which they were admitted. (McKeown 1976, 150).

What about the period since then? Standards of health have continued to improve in the last eighty years and it is natural to assume that this has been influenced by the growth of access to medical treatment, especially since 1948 when the NHS was established. The next section will consider the value of medicine in our own times.

The Effectiveness of Medicine in the Twentieth Century

What credit can doctors claim for their part in the continuing improvements in life expectation that have been achieved in the twentieth century? In attempting to answer this question, we come up against the problem of how to separate the possible contribution of medicine from all the other beneficial influences which have helped to reduce premature death by raising standards of health in the population. The case of falling rates of infant and maternal mortality illustrates these problems well.

Since the beginning of this century, there has been a continuous decline in the risk of death at birth for mothers and babies. There are a number of possible reasons for this trend. Of certain importance is declining fertility. The risks of childbirth for both mothers and infants increase substantially when the mother has already had several previous births. This suggests that falling family size is one of the most important reasons for reducing the risks of childbirth. Another important factor is diet. Infant survival is closely correlated with birthweight which is itself linked to the diet of the mother during pregnancy. This is a further beneficial effect of smaller households, their members are likely to be better fed for the simple reason that they are fewer in number. The research of Winter (see p.33) shows that between 1900 and 1930, infant mortality fell most sharply during the First World War (1914-1918). The most important reason was rising living standards in the poorest section of the community during the war, brought about by direct government intervention to ration food and control its price, to set minimum wage levels and to offer employment either in uniform or out of it. The most interesting of Winter's conclusions from the point of view of the present discussion is that medical treatment could not have made any positive contribution to the decline. This is because over 60% of the profession were in uniform. Some have inferred from this wartime shortage of medical care that the decline may have reflected a reduction in the use of instruments like forceps which often lead to birth damage. Whatever the truth of this, one thing is quite clear. In the first thirty years of the twentieth century, infant and maternal mortality rates fell most sharply at the time when the British population was starved of medical services because the majority of doctors had been 'drafted'.

How do we separate the effects of rising living standards, improved nutrition and reduced family size from other factors that might have helped to bring down mortality rates? Obstetricians have drawn on the evidence of decline to persuade governments that hospitalised childbirth is safer. This is despite the fact that there is no evidence to show that domicilliary childbirth (i.e. at home) carries more risk. In fact the opposite is true, the statistics show that babies born at home have a lower death rate. Doctors explain the greater safety of home birth by pointing out that more than 90% of babies are born in hospital including those most at risk. It is because only risk-free cases are permitted the option of a home delivery that they appear safer. The problem of testing the competing claims of the obstetrics lobby and those who support the call for more freedom of choice in childbirth is that it is no longer possible to carry out a test of which is the safer venue. This would involve the comparison of randomly selected mothers giving birth either at home or in hospital to see which is the safer. Because most births (over 95% in 1982) take place in hospital this test of effectiveness cannot be carried out.

If we look at the pre-war period, when most babies were born at home and when the mother being delivered in the maternity hospital was rather more likely to be from a higher social class, the evidence suggests that the hospital may well have been more dangerous. Death rates among rich women being delivered in hospital were actually higher than those of poor women being delivered at home! The trend of hospitalised childbirth has continued since then in the absence of any systematic evaluation of its relative effectiveness and without any attempt to test the ever more complex technological gadgetry applied to childbirth as part of the same process. So we do not know what part, if any, the machinery and drugs of modern obstetrics has played in reducing the risks of infant and maternal mortality although doctors are apt to claim credit for them. The same problem crops up when we look at other areas of treatment.

Intensive coronary care units for treating the victims of heart attacks were introduced into the NHS at great expense and without evaluation. Since then research has shown that the chances of recovering from a cardiac arrest are just as good, if not better, if the victim remains quietly at home in the bosom of family life. Nevertheless, the expansion of intensive care units in the NHS has continued. The reason that expensive methods of treatment come to be implemented without careful evaluation is that doctors are principally merchants of hope and their ethic is to try everything in their power to save their patients even if this involves new untested treatments. Even where it is clear that the chances of recovery are almost nil and where the treatment is more devastating than the disease, powerful therapies are still applied in the hope that 'this time it might just work'. In this doctors must often find themselves giving in against their better judgement to a desperate patient's need to try anything to keep hope of survival alive.

It would be wrong to suggest on the basis of this, that all medical treatment is useless. The problem is rather one of not knowing the relative merits or risks attached to different medical procedures and practices. This was the conclusion reached by Cochrane, in a book which called on his own profession to adopt a more scientific approach when introducing new forms of treatment. He argued that the value of most treatment routinely carried out in NHS hospitals had never been established and that consequently, doctors were more prone to act on the basis of 'medical opinion' rather than their knowledge of scientific fact. If so, this may go some way towards explaining why so few statistics are available to study the rate of recovery from various conditions among patients treated in NHS hospitals. The most striking example of this is the Hospital Inpatient Enquiry. This massive annual survey does not even bother to differentiate discharges where the patient is alive or dead.

In conclusion therefore, there is a shortage of evidence on which to reach a careful judgement about the contribution of medicine to general improvements in health in post war Britain. What we can say however is that medical science itself concedes that its theoretical knowledge of the aetiology (causes) of the two major diseases of the present day, cancer and heart disease, is underdeveloped. In each of these diseases the available medical treatment has a negligible impact on the chance of survival.

But if medicine cannot cure the major diseases of contemporary civilisation, what can be done about them? The realization that attempting to 'cure' degenerative disease is like trying to turn the clock back, has highlighted the importance of *prevention* and *care* in recent years.

Preventive approaches to health care are aimed at delaying the onset of disease by slowing down the ageing process of the human body. Preventive health care has little to do with the practice of medicine. It is much more concerned with the risks to health that are encountered in modern society, in diet, in work, in the environment and in behaviour. In some ways it constitutes a rediscovery of ideas widely prevalent at the turn of the century that the causes of disease are to be found in social arrangements and that social rearrangement is both possible and desirable if disease is to be prevented.

Growing recognition of the importance of *care* as opposed to *cure* is symbolised in such trends as the hospice movement. Hospices have been designed as places which provide a supportive and humane environment for the relief of pain in people suffering from incurable terminal disease. They have emerged in reaction to the impersonal and bureaucratic order of the modern hospital which is incapable of providing an environment where people can die with dignity and the support of their families. The aim of the hospice is to care for, not to cure the sick, reflecting a willingness to concede that medicine has no effective means of restoring health to many cancer patients. Similar 'winds of change' are blowing through the professional training of nurses.   The rediscovery that the vocation of nursing has its own particular contribution and is not merely an adjunct to medical treatment, is witnessed in the emergence of the *Nursing Process,* a new conceptual model for improving the quality of nursing care.

As yet, these trends could scarcely be said to present a fundamental challenge to organised medicine's control over the direction of health policy and the disbursement of national resources. 'High Tech' medicine with its emphasis on drugs, machinery and the drive to master disease remains the dominant feature of the NHS. The question of how the medical profession, despite its very limited record of achievement, became entrusted with the guardianship of the nation's health, will be taken up in chapter 7. In the present context, the question that remains to be answered is why the message that it is more useful to see the causes of disease as lying outside individuals in their living environments somehow got lost during the course of the last century as the emphasis on treating disease by treating the individual became the more prevalent approach.

Contemporary Medical Practice and the Bio-mechanical Model

What is contemporary medical practice like? The following brief summary may help to describe its principal features. Modern medicine is *cure* oriented. The primary goal is treatment and medical consultation starts with the description of symptoms. These are all the reported deviations from normal health, the clues needed for diagnosis and the application of the correct remedy. The patient's own feelings and impressions of what is wrong are less important than any organic signs that may be felt, observed or tested. If necessary, samples of the patient's body such as urine or blood may be taken or more complicated mechanical tests such as X-rays or ultra-sound scans might be carried out to find a medical label for the problem. The objective is the identification of organic causes beyond the patient's comprehension. This is why the sufferer's own account of what is wrong is largely irrelevant to diagnosis.

It would be unjust to suggest that doctors only treat the symptoms that patients bring to the consulting room. These may be only superficial signs of more serious underlying disorder. But by the time a patient consults a doctor, the option of prevention is already ruled out because the disease has advanced to the point of damaging the human body. Sometimes doctors are able to cure the patient by reversing the disease process. They may even be able to repair the organic damage by employing miraculous techniques which 'take the breath away'. Unfortunately, this is not a realistic possibility for most major degenerative conditions so that medical treatment can only hope to manage an irreversible disease by suppressing the continuing effects of its symptoms. From this it can be appreciated that medicine intervenes late in the development of disease. Doctors are not present when a disease starts, they wait for patients to present themselves for treatment. Consequently their primary interest is focused on the end point of the disease process not on its root causes. Like the efforts of witchdoctors, medicine is therefore primarily a pragmatic activity, oriented to answering the immediate needs of individual patients. This contrasts with its public image as a scientific activity oriented to the discovery of the true causes of disease.

Medical practice is also organised in such a way as to obscure clues about the root causes of disease. The doctor/patient relationship is highly confidential and surrounded by an atmosphere of anonymity. The preferred place of consultation or treatment is deliberately set apart from the normal living environment of the sufferer, thereby blinding the doctor to any clues it may contain about the causes of illness. Furthermore, since the content of consultation is ideally restricted to the description and examination of organic symptoms, information about the patient's social identity: occupation, marital status, workplace, income etc. only comes up incidentally, if at all.

From this brief summary of contemporary medical practice, a number of distinctive features stand out. They are as follows:

(1)   A dominant concern with the *organic* appearances of disease combined with a tendency to ignore, if not dismiss, the link between mind and body, between physical and mental well-being. Even psychiatry, the medical speciality devoted to mental illness,

predominantly seeks organic causes for the conditions it treats.

(2)   An orientation towards *cure*, towards the manipulation of organic symptoms with the intention of effecting their disappearance if at all possible. In this medicine shares certain parallels with magic and religion. All seek to perform their own style of conjuring trick.

(3)   A perception of *disease* as an autonomous and potentially manageable entity which threatens personal health in temporary or episodic fashion. Disease is the alien intruder which needs to be expelled. This is in contrast to the view of disease as an integral product of the person/environment relationship.

(4)   A focus on the isolated *individual* as the site of disease and the appropriate object of treatment.

(5)   A belief that the most appropriate place for treatment is a *medical environment*, the consulting room or the hospital, not the environment where symptoms arise.

These combined features of modern medicine have been summed up by some contemporary critics under the heading of the *bio-mechanical model*. This metaphor emphasises the shortcomings of restricting attention to the biological dimensions of disease and treating the individual sufferer as a mindless object whose physical body can be engineered like a machine. The doctor appears as a 'body mechanic', insensitive to the spiritual welfare of the patient, oblivious to the injury that medical treatment may itself inflict and ignorant of the wider environment in which disease originates.

McKeown's summary of the negative influence of the bio-mechanical model is as follows:

> Medical science and services are misdirected, and society's investment in health is not well used because they rest on an erroneous assumption about the basis of human health. It is assumed that the body can be regarded as a machine, whose protection from disease and its effects depends primarily on internal intervention. The approach has led to indifference to the external influences and personal behaviour which are the predominant determinants of health. It has also resulted in the relative neglect of the majority of sick people who provide no scope for the internal measures which are at the centre of medical interest. (McKeown 1976, XIV).

As he points out, the singular emphasis on the nuts and bolts of treatment pervades even the theoretical knowledge of medical science. This emphasis, perhaps inevitable in the consulting room or operating theatre, where the desperate patient needs immediate relief, quite wrongly dominates almost all medical research. University medical schools and research institutes, instead of searching for the fundamental causes of disease in the relationships between people, their behaviour and their environments, remain fascinated by the organic end-products of disease in human tissue. While their funds are used up on experiments into the chemical basis of inheritance or the immunological response to transplanted organs, major questions about how disease starts in the first place, are not merely left unanswered, they are not even asked. The result, in the words of one of the profession's own most celebrated scholars: '. . . almost none of the modern basic research in the medical sciences has any direct bearing on the prevention of disease or on the improvement of medical care'. (Sir Macfarlane Burnett 1971, 218).

These are devastating criticisms of medicine's approach to health in contemporary society advanced by some of the profession's own most respected members. They point to serious shortcomings in the ethos of medical science which are manifested in the organisation of medical research, in the training of doctors, and in everyday treatment. How could a misdirection of medical science on this scale come about?

Certain elements of contemporary medical practice arise necessarily in consultation and treatment and have probably been a typical feature of the relationship between healers and their clients from time immemorial. Among these we might include the one to one relationship, the emphasis on cure and the tendency to view illness as a temporary phenomenon. Like the client of an Azande witchdoctor, the typical patient has a pressing desire for the symptoms of illness to disappear. If treatment appears like a 'medical conjuring trick' this may have as much to do with the emotions of patients as with any deliberate design on the part of doctors. But some of the features identified above belong to a more recent phase of the history of western science. They are part of the legacy of two important developments: the 'Cartesian' revolution and the discovery of 'Germ Theory'.

How Medicine Mislaid the Real Nature of Health: The Mind Body Dualism and the Doctrine of Specific Aetiology

The 'Cartesian' revolution refers to the impact of the philosophy of René Descartes on social morality and via that on the development of science in the seventeenth century. Descartes insisted on the independence of mind and body. He saw the physical substance of the body as subordinate to the mind, a machine to be activated at the will of the human spirit. His ideas had a profound influence on the development of positivist science (logical thought based upon empirical observation) and they acted as a liberating force in medicine. Before Descartes and the advent of the *mind/body dualism,* the development of medicine was severely constrained by a religious embargo on the study of human anatomy. The orthodox Christian view held that body and soul were one and the same thing and, if the human body was not preserved intact, the soul could not ascend to heaven. As a result, human dissection was virtually impossible and without knowledge of anatomy, the development of medical science was severely retarded. Descartes paved the way for the development of a medical science oriented to the physiology of the human machine. The mind remained the seat of the soul, the province of religion while the body was handed over to new positivist science. In consequence, the foundations of medical science as it is practised today, were laid in the seventeenth century with an emphasis on the separation of physical and mental life which in its own way has been as confining as the influence of the medieval church on the physicians of pre-renaissance days.

The discovery of germ theory came much later and was itself a product of positivist science. It was discovered late in the nineteenth century through the research of Louis Pasteur in France and Robert Koch in Germany. Each succeeded in showing that infection occurs through the action of invisible micro-organisms. At the time, infective disease was still the major cause of death among all ages, as it had been for centuries. The orthodox medical view held that these diseases were caused by *miasmata* or bad air arising out of filth and lack of hygiene. Operating on this false premise, the sanitary reformers of Victorian England (see p.30) had implemented a series of public health measures which substantially reduced the risk of diseases like cholera and typhus. After Pasteur, the true nature of the infective process was understood. Infection does not arise spontaneously out of bad air but occurs though the invasion of one living organism by another. It happens when people eat infected food, drink infected water, get bitten by infected insects or animals and get close enough to inhale the infected air expelled through coughs and sneezes. The result is a struggle for survival between the human host and the virus (remember Darwin was around at this time too). In 1882, Robert Koch isolated and grew the tubercle bacillus in the laboratory. This meant that he could demonstrate that tuberculosis, the most virulent disease of the day with a reputation similar to cancer in our own times, was caused by a specific micro-organism. From this emerged the *Doctrine of Specific Aetiology:* a specific disease always has a specific cause.

This doctrine has been the most influential force in medical research for over a century. It implies that the way to understand disease is to create it in the laboratory and that the ingredients for explanation are found through minute observation of its bio-chemical appearances. In other words it proposes that the symptoms of disease tell their own story. Where Pasteur and Koch searched for the specific germs which caused each infective disease, medical scientists in laboratories all over the world today search for the specific *carcinogens* which they believe cause malignant tumours. Even the same idea of disease being caused by a noxious foreign body invading the healthy person, is retained.

The major shortcoming of this interpretation of disease applied as much in Koch's time as it does today. What Koch could not explain despite his ability to create disease at will in experimental conditions, was why *disease is rare, when infection is the norm.* To the city dwellers of nineteenth century Europe, lethal micro-organisms were no strangers. Most of the population would have been exposed to the tubercle bacillus and many probably retained the virulent infection in their bodies. Yet only a small proportion developed and suffered from tuberculosis. In fact during the course of his researches, Koch discovered that he had an immunity to TB which meant that he must have been exposed to the infection earlier in his life. Nevertheless he lived to a vigorous old age and died of a stroke. So the ability to create disease in an artificial environment, does not explain how and why the disease strikes living people in the real world outside the laboratory.

The arrival of germ theory has been hailed as a scientific revolution and many have concluded from this alone that it was responsible for declining mortality throughout the last century. But although they provided a reinterpretation of the major health problems of their day, the discoveries of Koch and Pasteur had no impact on the rate of death. The assumption that they did, arises from a confusion of pure knowledge and its application. Mortality from infective causes had been in steady decline for several decades before scientists were awakened to the existence of micro-organisms. The subsequent course of this decline was unaffected by the new knowledge. The reasons why health improved in the nineteenth century are the subject of the next chapter and we can only briefly anticipate them here. Death rates fell principally in response to rising living standards and to public health measures inspired by the movement for sanitary reform. The sanitary reformers, while they may not have understood the correct details of infective processes, knew well enough that their fundamental causes were poverty, overcrowding, and pollution. In 1849, John Snow, had proved that cholera was caused by impure water. He noticed that the risk of death from this disease was much greater in a part of London supplied with water by a particular company. By the simple expedient of removing the handle of the 'Broad Street Pump', he cut cholera death rates at a stroke and earned his place in epidemiological history.

Although germ theory filled in more accurate details of the transmission of infection, the basic proven methods of its prevention remained unaltered. Mortality from infective causes kept on falling at the same rate before and after the scientific breakthrough and it was to be another 70 years before effective treatment in the shape of penicillin was discovered. By then (1947), death from infection had become quite rare. So despite the ingenuity of Koch and Pasteur, the impact of germ theory on health has been limited. Its main influence has been on the theoretical development of medicine. In concentrating attention on the miniscule details of what disease does in the human body, Koch's *doctrine of specific aetiology* has deflected attention away from its *prior* causes in the environment and the individual's relationship to it. This is why modern medicine is dominated by the concern to explain and treat organic symptoms in individuals.

It also throws light on the removal of medical treatment from the patient's home to the consulting room or the hospital. In the nineteenth century most doctors treated their patients at home. Founded on charity, hospitals were primarily places of training where pauper patients received free treatment in exchange for acting as 'guinea pigs' for medical students. Those who could afford to pay were not eligible for free hospital treatment, and consequently it was stigmatised. In any case, before germ theory finally established the crucial importance of hygiene, hospitals had a quiet deservedly dangerous reputation. It took several decades to expunge the negative image of the hospital. The process was aided by germ theory in a number of ways. The most direct effect was on standards of hygiene and the realisation that infective patients constituted a risk to people suffering from other conditions. The isolation of contagious patients made hospitals much safer places. Furthermore, given the idea at the heart of germ theory that disease itself is best understood when isolated in laboratory conditions, it makes more sense to investigate symptoms in a specialised medical environment where tests can be undertaken in hygienic conditions. This helped to make the hospital more acceptable, even necessary for good results. As a further consequence, the process of diagnosis came to rely less and less on the verbal reports of patients and more and more on technological machine and drug-aided tests for symptoms. As Reiser (1979) shows, patients today have become objects in treatment, onlookers who may even be kept in the dark about what is happening to their bodies.

The combination of the mind/body dualism and the doctrine of specific aetiology have helped to shape the five principal features of contemporary medical practice identified on page 11: the emphasis on *(1) curing, (2) individuals of (3) episodic* bouts of *(4) organic* disorder in a *(5) clinical environment.* Some of these were reinforced rather than invented for the first time in the healing process. People suffering from an illness are inevitably predisposed to think of it as a temporary phenomenon and to seek out healers who are prepared to offer a cure. The concern with organic symptoms inside the individual and the rise of hospitals as 'high tech' disease palaces are newer features of the healing relationship. Their dominance in modern medicine may be due to the fact that they fit more easily with a curative focus. It is easier to treat one individual at a time and the reduction of illness to visible organic symptoms offers more scope for immediate remedial action. That patients attend doctors on medical premises in the present day rather than on their own home ground reflects the greater prestige of the profession and the growing, if somewhat misplaced, confidence of the public that effective cures are available.

Medicine as a Social Ideology

It is easier to see why medicine developed in the way it did than it is to explain the success of the profession in persuading us to believe in its version of what is good for our health. Public confidence in medical care has not been built on a sound record of achievement and it is in large degree nurtured by myths about the past. In the light of this it is easier to appreciate the role that medicine plays in contemporary society as *a social ideology.* In modern times doctors have taken over some of the social functions that priests played in the past officiating at birth and at death and determining the morality and ethics of human conduct in such spheres as reproduction and parent/child relationships. Medicine has become like a secular religion, a view reinforced by the knowledge that belief in its powers is based on myths about the past and faith in the present.

In portraying medicine as a social ideology, the intention is to stress that it should not be thought of as a body of scientific and apparently neutral truths about the nature of existence. Medicine presents an image of health which fits with the culture of industrial capitalist societies. The most important parallel is between the ethic of individualism in modern society and the focus of medical treatment on individuals. The modern way of life is more privatised and impersonal and these tendencies pervade all aspects of experience including health care. In these terms we can more readily understand why it is that medicine has become so influential in the determination of health policy in the advanced capitalist societies. Equally the reliance on machine technology and the belief that empirical science holds the key to human welfare both stem from the same self confident source.

This picture of medical science as a social ideology shaped in large degree by the social forces of our age, provides the rationale for the sociological study of health and of medicine. By demystifying the real process of how human health improved in the past and how it is promoted in the present, a whole new area of study is opened up. If medicine is not responsible, what is? This is the principal question addressed by the sociology of health. At the same time there is the question of how the medical profession succeeded in 'pulling the wool over everybody's eyes' including their own by all accounts. Explaining just how a profession succeeded in claiming the right to an exclusive monopoly of health care in the advanced industrial societies and with what consequences for human experience is the subject matter of the sociology of medicine. These questions will be addressed in the remaining chapters of this book.

Chapter Two

Human Health and Society

Health as the Product of Society

The evidence that health is the product of society rather than nature or medicine comes in a number of forms. To begin with there is historical evidence that patterns of disease change systematically over time in relation to social and economic development. We shall be reviewing this in the pages that follow drawing particular attention to the way in which the process of industrialisation eliminated the major diseases of the nineteenth century. This process was accompanied by the modern rise of population. Starting about 1830, the rate of death in Britain began to fall and it kept on doing so throughout the rest of the century. It led to a massive increase in the size of the population. The process was not confined to Britain although it does seem to have happened here first. But as methods of capitalist industrialisation spread elsewhere in Europe and beyond, population growth followed leading in the present day to the global population explosion.

The fall in the death rate occurred in all age groups and among both sexes. But it was most concentrated among females and, especially after 1900, among children. It had two effects. One is that the risk of death has become systematically linked to age, it increases as people grow older. Today a premature death is no longer, as it was in our great grandparents' day, that of a child. It is now a death before the retirement age of 65 years, an age which most people living before 1900 did not expect to reach. The other effect is the sexual division in the ageing population. The growing divergence of male and female life expectation means that after 65, there are almost twice as many women as men in the population. These demographic shifts have accompanied changes in occupational and domestic life. Women and children were gradually expelled from the workforce in the nineteenth century to become dependant housewives and schoolchildren. The coincidence of these events suggests that the influence of society on health includes the impact of changing age and sex roles. The following sections of this chapter will examine these demographic changes in detail and their possible causes.

Social Change and Patterns of Disease

As we saw in the previous chapter (p.4), the last 50 years has witnessed a gradual transformation of the profile of fatal disease. The direction and character of this change is illustrated in Figure 2.1. Figure 2.1 shows the distribution of death between different causes and by age. The most striking divergence between 1931 and 1973 is the virtual disappearance of deaths caused by infective disease. In the pre-war period this accounted for more premature death than any other single cause making up 40% of the total for both sexes before middle age. By 1973 they have almost disappeared from sight to be replaced among males by accidents and violence and among females by a combination of causes. Other distinctive changes include the reducing significance of respiratory illness especially among people below the age of 50, and the growing significance of cancer (neoplasms) particularly among women. In 1973 circulatory diseases (heart attacks and strokes) become the dominant feature of male mortality after the age of 30 accounting for well over 50% of the total. Among women, cancer is a more numerous cause in middle age although diseases of the heart and circulatory system become the chief cause of death in old age. There has been less change in the pattern of mortality among the elderly. In both periods the two major causes are the same, but they do not dominate the picture quite so much in the earlier period, accounting for about 60% of the total in 1931 and 80% in 1973 among people over 60.

These changes, which appear to have been gradually taking place during the pre- and post-war period in Britain were part of a much longer run change which began in the first half of the nineteenth century. Then infective disease accounted for an even larger share of total mortality especially among babies, children and young adults. They are often called the diseases of poverty because most of their victims were poor and malnourished. In contrast, the diseases that have taken their place in the twentieth century are called the diseases of civilisation or affluence. This is because they are thought to be the result of eating too much, taking too little exercise and abusing the body by smoking or drinking too much. They are also referred to as degenerative conditions, a term which links them to the gradual decay of the body's organs. An example is arterio-sclerosis, the 'furring up' of the arteries which carry the blood around the body. In plain language they imply that the human body is wearing out and it is ironic that they should be linked to a lack of moderation in consumption when they occur earliest among the section of the community who have the least income to spend.

Figure 2.1 Mortality by Cause, Age and Sex, 1931, 1973

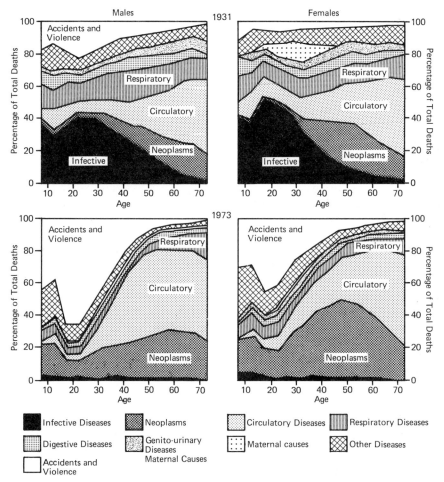

Source: OPCS *Trends in Mortality*. (HMSO, London, 1978). Reproduced with the permission of the Controller of Her Majesty's Stationery Office.

Today's major diseases are not new. It is of course extremely difficult to assess the relative contribution of different causes of death in the distant past. But fossil and bone remains suggest that the condition of arthritis, so prevalent from middle age onward in Britain today, is a form of suffering which unites our own experience with that of the early cave men and even the dinosaurs. The mummified remains of the pharoahs have proved to be a particularly valuable source for the investigation of disease among the ancients. From this source we find evidence of cancer, heart disease, pneumonia, kidney stones, cirrhosis, as well as a host of infections including many such as malaria, tuberculosis and schizosomiasis, which are still prevalent in Third World countries like Egypt, more than 2000 years later.

Nevertheless the comparative prevalence and severity of various diseases has changed greatly in the course of history and there is little doubt that in the centuries before 1900, infective disease was the main cause of death. Infection in human beings occurs when a bacterium or virus invades the human body. Although such organisms are by no means foreign to human beings, the arrival of a novel species creates a disturbance among the trillions already present causing an infection which could be fatal. If the individual recovers, future encounters with the same organism will be less severe because the body will have acquired an immunity. This is the reason why children were most at risk in the nineteenth century and before, and why today most infectious diseases like measles, chicken pox and whooping cough are childhood conditions to which the vast majority of adults are immune. However, in earlier centuries, as people from different continents met each other for the first time through voyages of exploration and conquest, unknowingly an exchange of micro-organisms also took place, often with literally devastating consequences. In these circumstances, when a previously unexposed population was introduced to an infection like measles for the first time, the result might be a catastrophic epidemic which was fatal for almost any contact irrespective of age.

The bubonic plague which wiped out about a third of the population of Europe in the space of little more than a decade of the fifteenth century, is a good example of this process. But equally instructive are the epidemics of smallpox which helped to destroy the populations and with them the civilisations of Central and South America (Aztecs and Incas) after the arrival of the Spanish conquistadors in the sixteenth century. According to McNeill, the population of central Mexico fell from 30 to 3 million in the space of less than 50 years from the time when Cortez and his hundred or so troops landed there and 'inaugurated epidemiological as well as other exchanges between the Amerindian and European populations'. As he wisely continues:

> In an age of almost world-wide population growth it is hard for us to imagine such catastrophies . . . Faith in established institutions and beliefs cannot easily withstand such disaster; skills and knowledge disappear. This indeed is what allowed the Spaniards to go as far as they did in transferring their culture and language to the New World, making it normative even in regions where millions of Indians had previously lived according to standards and customs of their own. (McNeill 1977, 205).

This is how infective disease contributed to the European conquest and colonisation of peoples and territories all over the globe.

In *Plagues and Peoples* McNeill describes how, in the centuries before 1800, the population of Europe developed a level of immunity to a variety of infections. In his words they became 'disease scarred'. Each century had a different disease. Leprosy in the fourteenth, plague in the fifteenth, syphilis in the sixteenth, smallpox in the seventeenth and eighteenth and tuberculosis and scarlet fever in the nineteenth. This epidemiological sequence gave Europeans a 'physiological superiority' which greatly aided their bid to colonise aboriginal peoples all over the globe. And, since disease was thought to be an instrument of divine will, it also gave the illusion of moral superiority: it was a sign that God was on their side when their enemies were wiped out by 'pestilence'.

Nevertheless, even among less susceptible European populations, mortality from infections remained high until the second half of the nineteenth century. From then on death rates began to tumble in a process known as the *modern rise of population.*

Health, Population Growth and Industrialisation

The nineteenth century witnessed many revolutionary changes of social organisation. These involved a spectacular growth of large towns and cities, the removal of work from the home to the factory, the growth of the state and of democratic politics and the beginnings of dramatic technological changes, which in the twentieth century would prove capable of putting men on the moon. Among these great transformations of human experience must be counted the modern rise of population. Figures 2.2 and 2.3 display the scope of the demographic revolution that began in the early decades of the nineteenth century.

Figure 2.2 The Modern Rise of World Population

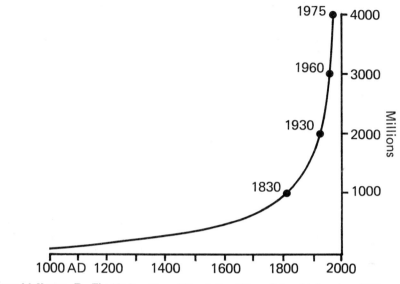

Source: McKeown, T., *The Modern Rise of Population,* Edward Arnold, London, 1976.

Figure 2.3 The Modern Rise of Population in England and Wales

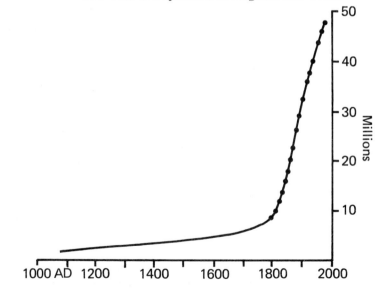

Source: McKeown, T., *The Modern Rise of Population,* Edward Arnold, London, 1976.

The increase of population that took place in the nineteenth century is called the 'Modern Rise' to distinguish it from previous periods of demographic growth. Unlike earlier periods when demographic increase was part of a cycle of growth and decline, the modern rise is unique because, as McKeown puts it, 'of its *size, duration and continuity'*. What this basically means is that it just went on rising and rising. Moreover it was not just a British phenomenon, it was global. How did it come about?

Population growth is determined by the combination of three factors, fertility, mortality and migration. Throughout the period in question, there was a net loss to the population of Britain from migration, so we may leave it out of any calculation of the reasons for population growth. Of the other two factors, some commentators, notably Wrigley and Schofield, have argued that the seeds of the modern rise were sown in the eighteenth century through an increase in fertility. But, since the period after 1870 has seen a fall in the birth rate, there can be little doubt that the most important mechanism of the change and its continuity is falling mortality particularly among the young.

The coincidence of:- (1) the modern rise of population; (2) the transformation of the nature of fatal disease; and (3) the rise of industrial capitalism constitutes powerful circumstantial evidence that the three processes are causally linked. Before we examine the evidence of their association and the possible directions of causal influence, we should first exclude one other possible reason for mortality decline. Is it conceivable that the human race, starting with the British, began to develop a spontaneous natural immunity giving protection from *all* infective micro-organisms? Could this be the explanation for the progressive disappearance of infective disease in the nineteenth and twentieth centuries.

We have already noted the way in which natural immunities develop in a population (p.22). Infections do not generally disappear completely, they usually survive as childhood diseases. But some are eliminated altogether. This happened to leprosy. Before 1400, it was an endemic disease in Britain, but then it disappeared from our shores and has never returned. But what needs to be explained in the nineteenth century is the disappearance not just of one infective condition, but all of them. Moreover these diseases which, even in a relatively immune population, survive to cause substantial mortality in childhood, no longer do so to anything like the extent they did in the past. And we must stress that the past means time immemorial. Infective disease has almost certainly been the main restraint on population growth since human beings first began to adopt a settled way of life thousands of years ago. If spontaneous natural immunity was the main reason for their sudden disappearance in the nineteenth century, we still need to explain why it happened when it did and not some time earlier.

The case of respiratory TB, the major cause of death during the period, provides a good example for illustrating the limitations of the natural immunity thesis. Because of population density, town dwellers developed more immunity to TB than people from the countryside. After 1830, the rapidly growing urban centres of Britain saw a continuing influx of rural migrants who ought to have been prime targets for infection. But instead of seeing an increased mortality from this disease amongst this unexposed rural population, the opposite occurred. The rate of death began to fall before the urbanisation process reached its peak and it kept on falling in the face of increasing migration from the countryside to the towns. So there can be little reason to conclude that the decline of TB was brought about by the development of natural immunity. If the resistance of the population improved it was more likely to be due to social or economic rather than natural causes.

Changes in the Risk of Death and the Social Division of Labour

The idea of *the social division of labour* was employed by the French sociologist Emile Durkheim to portray the source of reciprocity in social life. He wanted to explain how society could remain stable despite the tremendous social and economic upheaval of industrialisation. These changes meant the end of self sufficiency for the majority of households. Men, women and even children had to enter the expanding labour market to earn a wage to purchase the subsistence needs they previously produced directly for themselves. He argued that industrialisation created greater diversity in occupational life which might have been a source of social instability had it not also involved a higher degree of social co-operation. This was the result of the specialised nature of industrial production. Each firm produces only one type of commodity and people must necessarily enter into exchange relationships with one another to acquire the basic necessities of life. This promotes a network of interdependency with the market as its focal point.

The transition from a peasant household economy to a factory based industrial one did not occur overnight. In Britain, it gathered pace over several centuries in response to the enclosures of the land

and the introduction of capitalist methods of agriculture. In the nineteenth century the speed of change accelerated.

The redrafting of the social division of labour created a distinctive pattern of age and sex roles. This is what happened. In the first half of the century women and children were just as likely as men to be wage earners. But by the end of it they had been pushed out of the labour market via a programme of 'protective' parliamentary legislation which barred them from working underground and restricted their opportunities for factory work. Compulsory primary education (through a series of Acts from 1870), helped complete the process of turning adult males into breadwinners and females and children into their dependents. These changes, usually interpreted as part of a humanitarian struggle to improve the conditions of life of the working class, appear to feminist historians as evidence of the struggle between the sexes over rights to monopolise opportunities for paid employment.

The awful conditions of working class life whether in the factory or the home, had been brought home to the Victorian middle classes through surveys and reports like those of Edwin Chadwick, the Poor Law Commissioner. Through his surveys he came to believe that high rates of disease and death among working class parents and children were caused by their living conditions. Later, as an influential figure in the movement for sanitary reform, he drew on this knowledge to press for public health legislation. A primary aim of the factory acts was therefore to protect and promote maternal and child health. What was their impact?

One indication that the rise of the male breadwinner may have influenced the distribution of health, is found in the changing pattern of sex differences in mortality in successive periods since 1850. These are depicted in figure 2.4. Death rates by age are shown at 4 successive periods 1846, 1900, 1946 and 1973. At each period male death rates are expressed as a proportion of female rates.

There are only two instances in figure 2.4 when the female death rate is greater than that of males. These are in 1846 among 25-34 year olds and in 1896 among 5-14 year olds. These apart, the evidence points to a growing divergence in the risk of death between men and women which began sometime in the early part of the twentieth century and which has continued, opening up an enormous gap in early adulthood and middle age. These developments should not be interpreted as an increase of magnitude since 1946. In fact death rates for both sexes fell over this period. It is because the female rate has fallen faster and lower than the male rate that the gap between the sexes has widened so much.

Figure 2.4 Historical Change in the risk of Death for Males and Females throughout the Lifetime

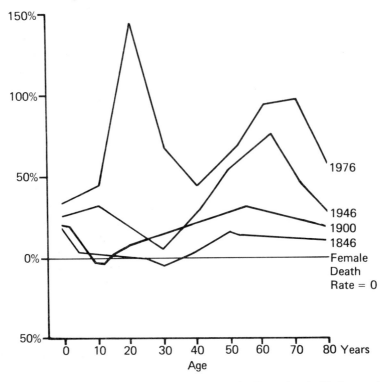

Source: OPCS *Trends in Mortality* (HMSO, London, 1978). Reproduced with the permission of Her Majesty's Stationery Office.

Is this picture the result of general social change and the recasting of male and female roles? The fact that the gap between the sexes was so much narrower in 1846, that it remained at the same level for the rest of the century, and then diverged so dramatically through the course of the twentieth century suggests that there is nothing 'natural' about the trend. If it were the product of genetic differences between the sexes then we might have expected more of a gap to be evident a century ago. So it looks as though the reason must lie in the changing social relationships of men, women and children.

A possible reason for these trends is the emergence of the male breadwinner and the retreat of his wife into domesticity. But even there things have not been static. Another important area of social change with direct implications for health, is the decline of marital fertility beginning after 1870. This had a direct impact on women's lives. It reduced the twentieth century family to a fraction of its nineteenth century size, transforming the routine experience of motherhood. In the last century this role involved a continuous cycle of pregnancy and childbirth which literally filled women's lives from marriage to old age. The reproductive career of a Victorian mother might involve a dozen or more pregnancies, several miscarriages and/or stillbirths and the quite likely prospect that one or more of her children would not survive infancy, childhood or adolescence. The expectations of her twentieth century sister could hardly be more different. With an average of only two children who are both likely to outlive her, a modern mother will complete her maternal duties well before she reaches middle age. This leaves almost half of her life still ahead for other social responsibilities. This change has come about through the desire for smaller families. It was made possible by changes in the moral climate surrounding contraception and by technological advances in the methods. The impact has been considerable both in improving standards of maternal and child health and in raising women's expectations of the part they may play in the social division of labour. Since the war the proportion of married women who work outside the home and whose wages contribute to the household income has risen to 60%. It is a trend that has done much to raise working class aspirations for home ownership as well as the means to pay for it.

These are fairly recent trends whose impact on sex differentials in mortality are yet to be felt. The situation before the Second World War was rather different. Then, apart from the war, the vast proportion of married women seemed content to remain at home. So it appeared that following soon after their expulsion from the labour market, the maternal dimensions of their roles were also diluted with beneficial effects on their health. Combined with the male monopolisation of breadwinner responsibilities, a fact later to be enshrined in welfare state and divorce legislation, this surely played some part in the growing divergence in the risk of premature death. The general picture then of improving health for both sexes but increasing inequality between them suggests that society influences health through the social division of labour and its gendered structure.

Standards of Living and Standards of Health

At the beginning of the twentieth century people were more sceptical about the value of medical treatment than they are in general today.

They could see more clearly why health was improving. Prominent social reformers like Beatrice and Sidney Webb had been alive in the nineteenth century to witness public health initiatives implemented often in the face of opposition from some sectors of the medical profession. Beatrice Webb had been one of Charles Booth's interviewers in his surveys of the labouring classes of London. Her experience had taught her that good health was built upon decent living standards not only in the form of adequate income, food, warmth, clothing and shelter, but also a clean and safe environment. This knowledge had been impressed upon the Victorian middle classes by the movement of sanitary reform. To them it was self evident that the maintenance of good health lay in high standards of public hygiene in the way of pure drinking water, efficient sewerage, safe working conditions, paved streets and highways and even public control over the standard of rented housing. These measures had gradually been implemented since 1834, culminating in the 'Great Public Health Act' of 1875. This legislative achievement was the reward for a 40 year struggle waged by people quite self conscious about their aim to make British towns and cities healthier places to live.

Today, we tend to equate the word sanitary with hygiene, but, strictly speaking, it is another word for health. Drawn from the latin 'sanitas' meaning healthy it is also linked to the word sanity. Sanitary reformers like Edwin Chadwick, who masterminded the 1842 *Report of the Sanitary Conditions of the Labouring Classes of Great Britain,* were pledged to the creation of healthy living conditions. One element was the provision of clean water and safe drainage, but other important goals were the reduction of overcrowding, the availability of work and free elementary education. The report contains a series of 'sanitary' maps showing a strong correlation between the social class of a district and its mortality rate. These maps reveal that the average age of death for the gentry was 42 years while for tradesmen and labourers it was 30 and 22 years respectively. Chadwick argued that the most effective way of reducing the poor rate, a tax levied for the support of the destitute, was to improve the health of the population and thereby reduce the numbers of unsupported widows and orphans. To this end he advocated new central powers to clean up the environment and supply clean water and safe drainage. His proposed reforms, like the 1834 *Poor Law Amendment Act,* in which he had also played a leading role, represented a high degree of state intervention in private affairs. Inevitably they invoked strong opposition. It was to be several decades before comprehensive public health measures of the kind he envisaged were implemented, and by that time the principle of state intervention in private life in the name of public health was well established. In the present day the same principle is even more powerful giving to public authority the right to intervene even in matters relating to the conduct of marriage and the treatment of children by their parents.

In the establishment of the singular importance of rising living standards for improving the health of the Victorian generation and its descendants, the work of one scholar stands out. The name of McKeown has already cropped up in this text. He is important in the debate about the causes of the modern rise of population for a number of reasons. He has brought together the empirical evidence and presented it in a particularly striking and accessible way. But equally significant, his critical assessment of the role of medicine has come from within the profession and has therefore been less liable to be dismissed as a 'doctor bashing' heresy.

McKeown's search for the major determinants of health in the nineteenth century is structured around an attempt to eliminate factors which were least likely to have made a significant contribution. Proceeding in this way he concludes that only three factors were important, nutrition, public hygiene and contraception. They were the principal agents in the decline of water- and food-borne plus airborne infections which formed 60% of the total reduction from 1850 to 1971. But, it is nutrition which McKeown picks out as having made the most significant contribution to the overall decline. He stresses that being well fed is the most effective form of disease prevention. This is seen today in less developed societies where vaccination programmes are not as successful as they should be because children are so malnourished. In effect he argues that the diseases we think of as the causes of death are really no more than an intermediate mechanism of high mortality resulting from food shortage and starvation.

McKeown concludes that the high mortality of the pre-industrial era was either the direct result of starvation or a function of decreased resistance to infection brought about by hunger and malnutrition. By 1900 the population of Britain was better fed through a combination of increased food production and a reduction of family size. This meant that the average household had more to eat and fewer mouths to feed. This explains how the spread of contraception, from 1850 onwards, helped to improve health. It also had a more directly beneficial effect on rates of maternal and infant mortality. Parity, i.e. the number of births in a woman's reproductive history, is strongly correlated to both rates. The more children a woman bears the greater the risks both for herself and the baby. Falling fertility probably made the most important contribution to improvements in survival prospects at childbirth.

McKeown goes further. He argues that much of the very high mortality of our own pre-industrial past was the direct result of starvation particularly among infants. In the absence of effective contraception, unplanned birth and unwanted children were commonplace. In such circumstances very high infant mortality must in some degree have been the result of parents being forced to neglect or even abandon babies that they could not afford to feed. The nineteenth century saw the growth of a concerted effort to save unwanted children through the creation of orphanages and foundling hospitals and by banning women from work. This was the publicly visible sign of a change in social morality encouraged by the increasing productivity of the British economy and the greater availability of resources to support human life.

Where did the resources come from? The answer to this question must undoubtedly be found in the rise of industrial capitalism. In the space of these pages we cannot enter into a discussion of why and how this economic revolution took place. But it is clear that the development of a fully fledged market economy in nineteenth century Britain, for all the human exploitation and social upheaval that it entailed, led to an enormous increase in human productivity and national wealth. The social distribution of the benefits of this economic miracle was very unequal but nevertheless it can hardly be disputed that by the end of the century the population in Britain was better fed, better educated and better clothed because of it.

Among the components of rising living standards, McKeown isolates diet as the principal determinant of increasing life expectation. But he also draws attention to the importance of improvements in communication, technology and hygiene as background factors which were necessary to enable the larger volume of food produced to be made available to the population in a state fit for human consumption. Nevertheless, his tendency to single out food as the principal reason for the reduction of risk to infection has led one observer to dub his approach as that of a 'nutritional determinist'.

This mild rebuke is issued by Winter, in an article which largely endorses McKeown's main thesis and which concerned to investigate the impact of the First World War on infant mortality. From 1914 to 1918, a period when the British economy was put on a war footing, the decline in infant mortality was greatly accelerated. In an examination of possible reasons, Winter concludes that it was the war itself, and its effects on the economy, that led to an above average improvement in the health of the population. There are three main grounds for this conclusion:-

(1) Access to medical care during the war years was greatly reduced because more than 60% of the medical profession was drawn into military service. For this reason it seems most unlikely that the recorded improvements could be due to medical treatment.

(2) Local authority services were cut back by the need to economise so that improvements to housing, sewerage and health clinics were at a standstill.

(3) Unemployment and casual employment among men were virtually eliminated, and women were drawn into the labour market in large numbers because of the extra demands of wartime production. This together with a whole host of other specific economic measures like rent control, food rationing and minimum wages in agriculture. introduced as part of the war effort, ensured that a substantial decline in poverty took place during these years.

His conclusion, that rising living standards amongst the poorest section of the community explains the precipitous fall in infant mortality, is reinforced by the fact that those same county boroughs of England, Wales and Scotland that registered the highest pre-war rates of infant mortality, experienced the greatest decline during the wartime years. These areas were concentrated in the industrial Midlands and the North containing urban areas with high concentrations of semi and unskilled manual workers. In the more affluent county boroughs of the southern England, the war made little impact on the course of infant mortality rates. The ironic conclusion therefore was that the health of the working class in this country benefited more from the 1st World War than it did from any other event in the first thirty years of this century.

Winter's analysis of why health improved shares much in common with McKeown. Both stress diet and rising living standards as the principal determinants of health. But Winter goes beyond this to emphasise wider societal mechanisms. For the period he studied the most significant of these was the interventionist role of the state in controlling the level of demand in the economy, the price of goods and services, the rationing of scarce commodities and the distribution of income. He deals with the period in which the scope for state intervention was enlarged as a result of the efforts of the movement for sanitary reform. The most important lesson from his work, is that access to work, to a stable and sufficient income, to decent housing, to family planning, to a clean environment and safe food and drink are more the product of government intervention than of individual initiative.

State Intervention and Human Welfare

The scope for government intervention to improve the health of the population was understood quite early in the nineteenth century as the struggle for sanitary reform testifies. The story of this movement illustrates the way in which the state came to assume a more direct responsibility for the lives of ordinary people. Sanitarianism represented the self confident beliefs of the Victorian middle classes that they possessed the right, the means and the power to shape their own and their fellow citizens' health. This was all the more significant as a social trend when one remembers that the movement developed in a society where the belief that God was the originator of life and decision maker about death, was still widespread. Preceding generations had accepted the ravages of disease as part of the normal order of human relationships with a divine authority. When Simpson introduced chloroform as an anaesthetic in childbirth in 1852, he was denounced from the pulpit. The pain of childbirth was the pre-ordained lot of mankind (or rather womankind). To prevent it was a sacrilege. As one clergyman of the time put it, 'Chloroform is a decoy of Satan, apparently offering itself to bless women, but in the end it will harden society and rob God of the deep earnest cries that arise in times of trouble, for help'. Simpson was accused of challenging the express command of the scripture 'In sorrow shalt thou bring forth children', and of usurping God's right to control life, death and the reproductive process. The same reasoning lives on in the continued opposition of Catholicism to contraception.

Strangely enough some of this self confidence has been eroded in contemporary times. The divine authority over human welfare today is not God, but the *market*. Those responsible for running our society have become fearful of interfering with the market mechanism which they see as a self-regulating phenomenon, best left to its own devices. This view is a throwback to a primitive phase of industrial capitalism. It denies the power of human beings to control their affairs through rational and intelligent methods, preferring the idea that a 'hidden hand' guides human beings to their material destiny. These ideas were quietly dispensed with by the Victorian middle classes. It remains to see how long their late twentieth century descendants will take to make the same discovery.

The recognition of the power of public authority to prevent disease was aided by, and helped stimulate, the development of statistics or 'political arithmetic' as it used to be called. This provided the knowledge for understanding the totality of disease, its distribution and its social correlates. Without this, there would be no grounds for rational public action. The series of sanitary maps in the 1842 report are an early example of these techniques used to accumulate evidence that would strengthen the appeal for public intervention. Armed with this innovative 'data base', Sanitarians like Chadwick, set out to persuade the government of the day that they could improve the health of the people by planned intervention in the environment. By 1875, as a result of their efforts, legislation had been passed which controlled the hours and conditions of work, ensured hygienic conditions in the production and sale of food and drink, empowered landlords to keep their tenancies in good repair, and local authorities to maintain high standards of public hygiene. These public health measures helped to create a healthy urban environment in Britain and they must be counted among the factors which raised the standard of living in this country before the end of the last century.

The concept of the standard of living therefore has two distinct dimensions. One consists of the personal resources available to individual households to provide for subsistence needs. The other comprises the social resources gathered and used by public authorities (central and local) for collective purposes. Political opinions differ as to the appropriate balance to be struck in dividing national income between private income and the 'social' wage. Those to the right of the political spectrum favour a redistribution of resources to private households letting them decide for themselves how much education or health care they need. Those to the left believe that this would lead to a deterioration of standards and to greater inequality and injustice. Whatever the virtues of these opposed perspectives, one thing that stands out from nineteenth and early twentieth century history is that the standards of health and welfare of the most vulnerable people in the community have risen most when the state played a more active and interventionist role in the economy and society.

This raises the question of the relationship between standards of health and the power of the state in different societies, one of the themes of the next chapter.

Chapter Three

Capitalism, Socialism and Health

Human Health and the Rise of Capitalism

The last chapter argued that human health was revolutionised by the development of industrial capitalism. Indeed the last 150 years have been the most dynamic period for human health in the whole of recorded history. Improvements appeared earliest in Britain, the first industrial nation, but they soon spread to other industrialising parts of the world. Today the modern rise of population is a worldwide phenomenon, a global explosion which, some people find as threatening to the future of humankind as a nuclear holocaust. The material fruits of capitalism, measured by rising living standards and improved life expectation, are not equally shared. Enormous inequalities exist between different nations in the developed and the less developed world and between classes within individual nation states (see chapter 4). Even so, industrial capitalism ushered in new material conditions for human life witnessed in population growth on a scale never previously encountered.

How did industrial capitalism revolutionise human health? Marx provided the answer to this question when the new economic system was still in its infancy. He recognised its enormous potential for expanding the productivity of human labour and for bringing the forces of nature under human control. Marx had a love/hate relationship with the capitalist economic miracle. He saw clearly and prophetically its progressive character, but he also knew that while for some it represented civilisation, for others it equalled class exploitation. Marx anticipated that capitalism would ultimately give way via a process of class struggle, to a socialist version of industrial society. Socialism would retain the best features of capitalism while sweeping away its exploitative class structure. The private ownership of productive property would be abolished, leaving the workers' state to control the use and allocation of economic resources in the interest of everyone. The standard of health of the whole population would then be raised to that enjoyed by the ruling class because protecting health would be a fundamental goal of socialist industrialisation, replacing the profit motive as a means of gauging the value of human labour.

Has Marx's prophecy come to pass? In general the answer is no. Since the First World War, his model of political economy has inspired the formation of a number of socialist industrial states in Eastern Europe, although the manner of their appearance has not been exactly as he envisaged. They have generally been born in a pre- or early capitalist phase of development and inaugurated by war rather than through explosive economic contradictions. In each of these societies, the power of the state is much greater than it is in the liberal democracies of Western Europe and North America, and central planning has replaced the market in the allocation of scarce resources. At the same time the original capitalist states have themselves introduced substantial reforms. Like their Eastern European neighbours, societal reform has been stimulated by the events of war as much as through economic struggles between classes. The effect of the two world wars in the twentieth century on the politico-economic map of Europe, has been to bring about social revolutions in the losing nations while promoting welfare state systems among the victors. In Britain the development of the welfare state was largely the product of the second world war. During the 1920s and 30s the shortcomings of market capitalism were revealed in stark fashion with mass unemployment and deteriorating living standards providing almost perfect conditions for organised labour to rise up and overthrow the system. Yet, compared to the war years of 1939-45, this was a slack period for reformist legislation. It was at the height of hostilities in 1942 that the Beveridge report appeared with its detailed design for a comprehensive welfare state including full employment, an overhaul of secondary education, the national health service and the social security system.

Health in Contemporary Capitalist and Socialist Societies

So the historical events of the twentieth century gave the modern world a number of more or less capitalist and more or less socialist states in various stages of economic development. All vary internally in the degree of social and economic inequality and in the comprehensiveness of their welfare legislation. In general those societies which have retained the market as the means of allocating economic resources have been more successful in raising living standards. This is reflected in higher standards of health. Even so within the category of welfare state capitalism there are marked variations. At one extreme is Sweden with the lowest infant and adult mortality rates anywhere, the product of wide ranging and generous welfare provision. At the other is the United States, where mortality rates would be much lower were it not for massive social and economic inequalities between black and Hispanic and white Americans perpetuated by the relative absence of comprehensive welfare state provision. Even so, by 1975, the US recorded lower overall mortality than England and Wales despite the latter's more developed welfare provision.

Table 3.1   Trends in Mortality in Selected Industrial Societies

Country	1916	1926	1936	1946	1956	1966	1971-5
Czechoslovakia	316	248	180	152	109	108	108
Hungary	367	265	201	167	118	107	108
Italy	314	225	184	133	108	96	90
Japan	385	358	334	197	129	97	84
Spain	386	274	264	160	110	92	90
Sweden	170	137	125	103	89	82	73
UK (England & Wales)	222	167	146	114	102	97	93
USA	255	192	156	97	102	98	90

Source: Adapted from *International Mortality Statistics*, Alderson 1981. Based on SMRs (all
persons) calculated from a base of England and Wales 1951-1975 = 100.

Table 3.1 compares mortality trends in a number of countries since 1916. Czechoslavakia, Hungary, Italy, Japan and Spain are included to represent a variety of market and planned economies in the present day whose mortality rates at the beginning of the period were broadly similar. They therefore provide some clues on the impact of different pathways to industrialisation on health. Sweden, USA and the UK are included to show variation between the mature capitalist societies. The evidence suggests that societies which have retained the market as the means of organising economic production have experienced more substantial reductions in mortality, especially since the war. Take for example Czechoslovakia and Italy. In 1956, the mortality rates of each stood at 109 and 108 respectively. By 1976 the rate in Czechoslovakia remained static while that of Italy had fallen to 90. Even more striking is a comparison of Hungary and Japan. In 1956, their rates were 118 and 129 respectively. Twenty years later the relative position was reversed following a dramatic fall in Japanese mortality. There can be little doubt that this trend is closely associated with the spectacular growth of industrial capitalism in Japan.

Is Modern Capitalism bad for your Health?

These trends indicate that health is primarily the product of social and economic development. Since the highest living standards have been achieved in contemporary capitalist societies, this is where people enjoy the highest standards of health. Nevertheless some writers insist that the capitalist version of industrialisation is extremely harmful to health. Drawing on Marxist concepts and categories, these critics assert that the capitalist mode of production damages health in two specific ways. First they point to the dangers inherent in capitalist commodities themselves and in the manner of their production. The very goods and services which contribute to high living standards, together with modern methods of production, are held up as sources of health risk in themselves. It is alleged that people are led to desire and therefore to consume hazardous goods like refined and processed foods, cigarettes and motor cars because they are profitable. The implication is that healthy commodities are less profitable and could be manufactured with less risk to health.

The second target is the manner in which the capitalist labour market erodes social relationships based on kinship, neighbourhood and community. This occurs through the necessity for the labour force to be semi-nomadic, obliged to move wherever work is to be found. This negative theme is reminiscent of Louis Wirth's image of the rootless and anonymous state of humanity in modern urban communities.

In these critiques, the process of class exploitation in mature capitalism does not take the form of what Marx called immiserisation: ruthless profiteering at the expense of wage levels and living standards. This process, called absolute exploitation, belongs to an earlier more primitive phase of competitive capitalism where small enterpreneurs struggle with one another for a larger share of the market. In the advanced capitalist societies characterised by large monopoly corporations, exploitation takes a relative form. It consists of the imposition of methods of organising work which are alien to human beings and of commodities which do more harm than good. The latter theme, which draws on the Marxist concept of *commodity fetishism,* has the unfortunate tendency of depicting ordinary people as the dupes of capitalist advertising, unable to recognise their real material interests and dependent on radical intellectuals for a true understanding of their basic needs. Let us examine each of these two themes in more detail.

The first theme has a number of strands. The goods produced by capitalist industrialisation constitute one set of risks to health. Many popular capitalist commodities are said to be not useful and some positively lethal. High on the list of offenders are tobacco products. The mass consumption of cigarettes is perpetuated despite the established health risk through largely uncontrolled advertising. Other dangerous commodities include some everyday staples such as white bread and artificial baby milk. They constitute health risks because they are highly processed, the result of modern methods of production. These regressive features of commodity production under capitalism come about because exchange value dominates use value in determining what goods and services will be produced. The foods available on the supermarket shelf are there not because consumers prefer them to healthier alternatives but because they have higher profit margins. Thus capitalism is responsible for a diverse range of modern 'ills' from obesity to women's desire to liberate themselves from breastfeeding.

A second set of risks is encountered directly in the form of industrial injuries and diseases and indirectly through the dehumanising nature of work itself. It is argued that they are worse under capitalism because productivity is measured by the profit motive and not by criteria which include the welfare of workers. The dehumanisation of work occurs through the substitution of machines for human skill leading to a deskilling of the workforce. Even worse is shiftwork necessary to keep the machines going night and day. As a result, work carries no intrinsic satisfaction. It becomes no more than a means of earning a livelihood. On the other hand, being out of the labour force is also seen as a source of deprivation. Doyal and Pennell in *The Political Economy of Health* depict housework as a deprived form of work because it is menial on account of being 'undercapitalised and isolated' (p.74). What the term undercapitalised means is unclear. One interpretation would be that there is a lack of machinery to substitute for human labour. This however, would stand in contradiction with arguments elsewhere in the same text linking deskilling to the very same process. The argument is unsupported by empirical evidence, which makes it difficult to take issue with it. However it is hard to agree with the claim that the modern home is undercapitalised. Trends in personal consumption in the last decade would point to the opposite conclusion, showing working class households striving to both own and improve their own homes. Home improvement firms have been a growth area of capitalism and household commodities like built-in kitchens, washing machines and freezers have been acquired by more and more families. In these circumstances it seems that housework in modern times is only menial where the household is poor and cannot afford the modern housewives' basic tools. From this perspective it is difficult to sustain the image of depressive illness as the occupational disease of housewives brought on by the repetitive, isolated, exhausting and demoralising task of looking after home and children. More persuasive and closer to the empirical reality would be a linkage of poverty and powerlessness as sources of stress-related symptoms in housebound women.

The other charges against the capitalist mode of production in the sphere of work, are less clearly linked to capitalism. Tendencies to fragment the production process and to substitute machines for human labour are a feature of industrialisation as a whole and it is not clear that a transition to socialism would necessarily make work processes themselves any more intrinsically satisfying. Moreover it may be that some of the most important features of modern occupational life are underestimated in Marxist accounts. This is revealed, for example, in the dual attitude to labour force participation among women and men. For women paid work represents a solution to 'housewife blues', yet for men it equals alienation, boredom and a psychological if not a physical health risk. What is underestimated is the importance of work for both sexes as a means of participating in the public sphere of society, of being *seen* making a contribution to the division of labour and to the process of production itself. The wage packet and access to a job may be as important as symbols of social citizenship as they are of direct material benefit. This maybe why women themselves have come to perceive of entry to the labour market as a means of personal liberation. The post-war era has seen a steady growth in female participation and today more than 60% of married women work for wages outside of the home. This suggests that there is no functional link between the oppression of housewives and the capitalist market making it incorrect to see female depression as an occupational disease *caused* by capitalism. Some might go even further and argue that under capitalism, the liberation of women has gone further than it has in any previous form of civilisation. Certainly in terms of life expectation women have benefited disproportionately to men.

The idea of work as a symbol of social participation owes much to Durkheim's model of the social division of labour as the principal mechanism of social integration in modern society. From this perspective it is immediately evident that unemployment would constitute a threat to health. This is another theme in the portrayal of capitalism as a threat to health. The fact that rates of mortality and unemployment tend to rise and fall together adds weight to this idea and a number of studies have sought to investigate it. Fox and his colleagues offer strong evidence linking job loss to increased mortality among both breadwinners and their wives but it is unclear how this comes about. Brenner argues that unemployment causes stress-related disease because it is a disruptive life event (see p.83). Stern and others have contested this, showing that those at risk of unemployment are the same people who are at risk of premature death because of their poverty. They argue that it is the poverty rather than the stress caused by unemployment which increases mortality risk (see p.93). In either case it is likely that an unfettered system of free enterprise capitalism would cause the rate of unemployment and of poverty to fluctuate in accordance with market forces. In such circumstances unemployment as a cause of stress or poverty-related disease can be directly linked to capitalism. However unfettered market forces are not inevitable. To assert otherwise is a misconstruction of both Marxism and Thatcherism. Since the Second World War, most capitalist societies have sought to regulate the level of unemployment through a variety of Keynesian economic policies. As a result the volume of unemployment tolerated, along with the level of social security paid to the jobless, are both matters of political choice subject to the decision of the ballot box. If a minority of unskilled and semi-skilled people can be made to bear the brunt of economic recession or industrial restructuring, why should the survival of capitalism be threatened? The welfare of the weakest members of the society depends on the compassion of the rest of the electorate and on the skill of political parties in representing their case. In these circumstances allocating blame for the insult of unemployment is complicated by political and ideological considerations and cannot be simply reduced to being an inevitable or unmanageable feature of the capitalist mode of production. The wide inequalities in health in advanced capitalist societies do not take the form of a simple polarised division between haves and have nots. As chapter 4 reveals, they take the form of relative deprivation, a series of layers of advantage and disadvantage which do not provide a clear basis for collective identification and action. For this reason a specifically Marxist analysis of class offers no more insights on the causes of inequality in health than any other sociological model.

Is Socialism any Healthier?

The argument that the profit motive increases the risk of industrial accidents and injuries is surely correct. Many industrial processes are inherently dangerous and some should probably be banned altogether. If the relationship between an industrial disease or injury can be established, then a worker or a union can use the courts to gain compensation. In these circumstances the market itself may outlaw the production of certain commodities because the cost of compensating victims makes the enterprise unprofitable. This has been the fate of asbestos companies in the United States. But for most industrial diseases, the risks are not established as clearly as for asbestosis, making the market effects of legal compensation an ineffective mechanism for protecting workers' health. Nevertheless the influence of market forces in determining the health risks of work should not be overstated. Since 1900 the incidence of industrial accidents has fallen considerably and comparisons between contemporary capitalist and socialist states in the modern world do not suggest that market forces encourage more accidents than the forces of central planning. Table 3.2 provides evidence of mortality risk from a number of causes in Czechoslovakia, Hungary, Italy and Spain selected because of their similar levels of economic development in the pre-war era. The UK data is given as a point of reference.

Table 3.2   Selected causes of death in some contemporary industrial societies, 1971-75

Country	Czechoslovakia	Hungary	Italy	Spain	UK (England and Wales)
All causes	108	108	90	90	93
Lung Cancer	200	148	140	97	222
Stomach Cancer	195	218	161	151	117
Circulatory Disease (males)	128	238	98	107	102
Accidents (males)	240	230	200	179	119
Accidents (excluding traffic)	242	236	136	177	102
Suicide	240	374	59	46	76

Source: Adapted from *International Mortality Statistics,* Alderson 1981. SMRs derived from a base of England and Wales, 1951-1975 = 100

Each of the causes in table 3.2, has a higher incidence in the planned economies of Eastern Europe. The one exception is the elevated risk of lung cancer in the UK, one of the few areas where Britain still leads the world. The causes are chosen to represent the so-called diseases of civilisation which Doyal and Pennell link to the consumption of capitalist commodities. It is clear however that the chances of dying from circulatory disease or lung cancer are no less in Czechoslovakia or Hungary suggesting that exposure to risk factors in diet and smoking is much the same in all industrial societies regardless of their political character. Furthermore the higher rate of accidents among men under Eastern European socialism offers no support to the argument that the workplace is safer in societies where the central planning bureaucracy has the opportunity to treat occupational health as a major priority of the productive process. Why is this so?

The most probable answer is the drive to industrialisation in socialist societies. Translated at factory level into a race to meet central planning goals, this pressure on the production line may be just as destructive to human health as the profit motive in capitalism. Another factor likely to be of major importance is the absence of participatory democracy as a means of safeguarding the workplace and the environment. In Western Europe and North America, this is achieved through the activities of political organisations, pressure groups and trade unions. In Eastern Europe, there is less countervailing power to regulate the activities of those who control the means of production and this may help to explain the greater risk of accidental death (see Table 3.2).

Individualism, Stress and the Capitalist Way of Life

The other theme in the Marxist critique is that the capitalist way of life is stressful. This is because it is highly individuated. The labour market is oriented to individuals not to families or kinship groups and because people are forced to leave their communities in search of work social networks and ties binding people together are destroyed.

> The basic social process of capitalism is itself the source of increased stress. The very same social changes which increased agricultural productivity and made possible a large non-agricultural labour force are also the fundamental causes of the health risks that increase with capitalism. These changes can be summarised as the uprooting of people from stable communities and the subjection of life to the constantly changing demands of the market for labour. (Eyer 1984, 28).

This assessment of social disorganisation under capitalism is reminiscent of Durkheim's concept of anomie: the breakdown of the normative structure of relationships in the transition from mechanical (pre-industrial) to organic (industrial) social solidarity. It was a feature of the capitalist mode of production which Marx particularly admired. The destruction of traditional paternalistic ties binding people to particular communities was for him one of the pre-conditions for the growth of a new *social* consciousness. However research on diseases of stress (see p.80) suggests that social support is important in the maintenance of self esteem which in turn enables individuals to handle stressful experiences without ill-effect. The problem is how to create social support outside of the enduring bonds of kinship or community of birth.

Another dimension of stress induced by capitalism is the encouragement of individualistic, selfish attitudes in which people are only concerned with the acquisition of material possessions. This egotistic and materialistic orientation to life further serves to undermine the individual's access to social support. The role model for this is the so-called *type A personality,* particularly prone to coronary disease. This personality type has not been found to predominate among stroke and heart attack victims in Britain, although research indicates that it is prevalent in the USA (see p.88). Eyer argues that the rise of possessive individualism and the destabilisation of traditional communities explains class differences in health, rural/urban differences and the relationship between rates of mortality and the changing rate of unemployment.

There is a fundamental flaw in this argument stemming from a failure to examine the empirical realities of disease and premature death in modern capitalist societies. The sort of person held up as the most likely victim of disease, the striving materialistic nomadic worker, has better than average chances of surviving to retirement age and beyond. Those at the greatest risk of early death are people in social class IV and V, whose occupational prospects scarcely make it either worthwhile or even possible for them to kick over the traces and seek their fortunes in a new locality. In contemporary Britain the highest death rates are found among low paid manual workers whose major resource is likely to be the tenure of a council house which ties them to a neighbourhood for life (see p.55). Their health is principally at risk through long term economic deprivation, the product of being stuck on the lowest rung of the socio-economic hierarchy.

The general impression left by Marxist writers is that capitalism is disastrous for human health. The argument is advanced from the position of a socialist utopia undefined beyond the identification of certain negative features of capitalism such as the profit motive that would be abolished. From this hazy perspective, capitalism is treated as a blanket category with no account being taken of the substantial differences between contemporary market societies in standards of health and welfare provision. Doyal and Pennell develop their case through a process of theoretical logic which is only reinforced by evidence where it fits the desired construction of reality. Hostile evidence is avoided. There is no reference to the societies of Eastern Europe which have attempted the socialist experiment. Not even the usual disclaimer of modern Marxism that these societies have nothing to do with the kind of socialism Marx anticipated. This means that an opportunity to use material relating to alternative models of industrialisation (where the market has been eliminated) is missed. This partiality of approach belongs to an analysis primarily oriented to political persuasion rather than to understanding the real nature of the relationship between health and societal development. It is further reflected in the imbalance of the critique as a whole. Doyal and Pennell do not concede that many of the commodities of advanced capitalism are very beneficial and have transformed human experience in positive ways. Instead everything is lumped together in equally negative terms. Eyer commits the same mistake when he implies that the destruction of traditional close knit communities and the freeing of the individual from the interpersonal ties of kinship and community is a wholly negative process. What he fails to recognise is that these very same communities have operated cruel restrictions of personal freedom and development. If capitalism has helped to break up stifling and repressive social norms such as those surrounding the oppression of women, this may be one of its finest achievements.

Utopian Models of Health

The singular emphasis on the negative dimensions of contemporary capitalist civilisation, unites the Marxist perspective with the anti-industrialisation stance of Ivan Illich. Illich picks on over-industrialisation, not capitalism as the principal cause of ill-health in contemporary society. The main butt of his attack is medicine and in his book *Limits to Medicine,* he identifies three ways in which modern medicine is pathogenic to human health. His theme is *iatrogenesis* meaning something having its origin (genesis) in doctors (iatros). Its three forms are clinical, social and cultural. Clinical iatrogenesis constitutes the risks to health contained within medical treatment itself: the application of dangerous experimental techniques, the prevalence of unwanted side effects, medical drug addiction and treatments that are more painful and disfiguring than disease itself. Social iatrogenesis refers to the wider influence of medical ideology in society at large, to the process whereby diverse areas of human experience such as birth and death have become medicalised. In the medicalisation of social problems, their political nature is stripped away as they become neutral objects for technological treatment. Cultural iatrogenesis is the process whereby individuals relinquish the will to take care of themselves to professional experts. It results in a form of personal paralysis, a loss of control and of self confidence in dealing with a whole range of personal and emotional problems. Via these three forms of iatrogenesis, Illich accuses medicine of expropriating health for selfish professional interests. This is what constitutes the major threat to health in advanced industrial societies.

His critique is part of a wider reaction against the dependence of modern society on science and technology and the neglect, even abandonment, of spontaneous natural human capacities. Human beings have lost control over their destiny and even the natural environment of the world is at risk from the technological monster out of human control. The remedy proposed is a retreat from advanced industrial society to small scale intimate communities liberated from the tyrannies of machine, factory, bureaucracy and scientific expertise - back to a world where human beings experience direct control over their circumstances and destinies. No detailed proposals for the reconversion of the massive urban communities of the modern world are offered.

There are several parallels between Illich and Marxists like Eyer and Doyal and Pennell. Both emphasise negative dimensions and neglect the dialectical interplay of good and bad in the modern way of life. In each there is a strong theme of dehumanisation; alienation for the Marxists, expropriation for Illich. The reactions against advanced technology and machines usurping natural human capacity and skill is common to both. It implies that a return to an earlier technological phase of economic life would represent an improvement in the human condition. Allied to this is the idea of false needs. Human beings are seen as being tempted, bought off, by commodities which do them more harm than good. Finally both Eyer and Illich react against the urban migration promoted by industrialisation. They share the view that people would be better off if they stayed put in small scale, close knit communities. What seems to unite these two pessimistic accounts is an element of romantic idealism. Each promises a vision of better health under new social conditions — de-industrialisation for Illich and socialism for the Marxists — but neither offers any guidance on how their model societies could be made a reality.

Despite the common ground, Marxist writers specifically reject the views of Illich. Navarro in a spirited challenge, accuses him of mistaking industrialism for the pattern of class dominance in capitalist society. He argues that the road to better health is paved with the process of democratic control over the productive system. But although, he carefully avoids much of the romantic idealism of fellow Marxists, he does not specify how his model of democratic socialism would work. The unanswered question is how a complex industrial economy can be controlled and managed by everybody without bureaucratic power structures. In other words, he does not face up to the problem posed by Max Weber, that bureaucracy is the fundamental mechanism of legal rational authority and the most pervasive form of power in modern society. In particular he does not answer Weber's challenge that bureaucracy is even more of a constraint in socialist society where public officials rule in the name of collective welfare.

Concluding Remarks

Let us be clear in concluding this chapter that the capitalist mode of industrialisation is far from perfect as a form of social organisation and there are many ways in which it is corrosive of human health. Among the different varieties of welfare state capitalism that exist in the world today some are far more effective than others in promoting and protecting human health. Equally amongst the same family of capitalist nations, levels of social and economic equality or social citizenship vary considerably. But whatever its shortcomings there are no signs to indicate that the majority living under the capitalist version of industrial society would wish to roll back the tide of either capitalism or industrialisation. Consequently there is a credibility gap between the vision of human welfare presented by writers like Illich and Doyal and Pennell and the everyday experience of real people. The picture they draw makes it difficult to see why the Western working class have put up with capitalism for so long given the damage it is supposed to do to their health. The reason for the continued popularity of the capitalist system, is that the majority of people do quite well out of it. They know from direct experience that living standards have improved and this may be why they are unwilling, in the absence of more persuasive reasons 'to sacrifice a bird in the hand for two in the bush'. In Marxist terms their pragmatism is an example of false consciousness: a sign that people do not realise their true material interests because the exploitative nature of capitalism is obscured by ideological processes. In Marx's own day, religion was the opium of the people, today it is medicine. In this way, Marxist critics create a further problem for explanation. How does capitalism mystify its negative effects on health? How, in particular, does it succeed in retaining popular loyalty despite all the suffering it causes? This theme, prominent in the work of Navarro, we will leave to chapter 7.

Chapter Four

Social Inequalities in Health

The Duration of Life as a Measure of Social Welfare

We have seen how the development of industrial capitalism in Britain in the nineteenth and twentieth centuries was associated with a continuous decline in the death rate and consequently with an increase in the average length of life. This represents an improvement in human health, brought about by the process of industrialisation and the social and economic changes which it entailed. It means quite literally that human bodies are more durable than they used to be and that people consequently tend to live longer than their parents or grandparents. Improvements in health are thus embedded in the general rise in living standards which began in the nineteenth century and which continued at an accelerating pace in the twentieth.

This extension of the length of life is the best measure of health available (see p.3) and it is also a good indicator of *social welfare.* This last point deserves special emphasis. We have seen in chapter 2 that the increased life span of British people in the twentieth century is a product of a change in the way society is organised. It is therefore a form of welfare produced by society: hence the term *social* welfare. This leads to an obvious sociological question: how equally is this particular form of social welfare i.e. health, distributed among the British population? The answer to this question is found through an examination of social inequalities in health and it is worth emphasising that the existence of differences in health between socio-economic groups, shortly to be examined, is further evidence of the fact that health is a product of society.

The Measurement of Social Inequality in Health

The analysis of social inequality is a predominant concern of sociology and social class is without doubt the discipline's master concept. But sociologists differ in the way they use this concept. Some employ it in a purely theoretical way to convey the nature of social conflict as a force for societal change. Others use it as a distributional measure. They divide the population into a series of layers each representing different degrees of social and economic power. In this book social inequalities in health will be examined in the latter sense, as a hierarchical distribution of advantage and disadvantage. We will employ the Registrar General's classification of social class. This choice is largely dictated by the form in which the official statistics of mortality are published. Every decade the Registrar General (RG) carries out a study of variations in mortality among people engaged in different occupations. These data have provided the most clearcut evidence of the extent of social inequality in health. The RG's social class sorts all the occupations in the labour market into six broad groups arranged hierarchically according to their 'social standing in the community'. It is therefore a measure of occupational class. Although, as critics often observe, the basis of the classification has never been systematically evaluated, it has proved to be a remarkably powerful discriminator of life chances not only among male wage and salary earners but also among their wives and children. It is made up as follows:-

Social Class		Percentage of Workforce (1970)
I	Professional e.g. Doctors, Lawyers	5%
II	Managerial and Lower Professional e.g. Teachers, Sales Managers	18%
IIIN	Non-Manual Skilled e.g. Clerks, Cashiers	12%
IIIM	Skilled Manual e.g. Bricklayers, Underground Coal Miners	38%
IV	Semi-Skilled e.g. Bus Conductors, Postmen	18%
V	Unskilled e.g. Porters, Ticket Collectors, General Labourers	9%

In this scale, there are three manual and three non-manual classes. It would be possible to analyse health inequalities between two classes: manual and non-manual workers. However to do so would be to obscure the substantial differences which are found within these two broad categories as the following pages will indicate.

The Extent of Inequalities in Health

Official statistics for England and Wales clearly indicate that the

MERTHYR TYDFIL COLLEGE
LIBRARY

risk of premature death is systematically related to social class (cf. OPCS 1978). Inequalities are found at birth, in childhood and adolescence and throughout adult life. Figure 4.1 illustrates the consistent way in which the Registrar General's scale identifies the pattern of class differentials in mortality.

Figure 4.1 Mortality by Social Class, Age and Sex

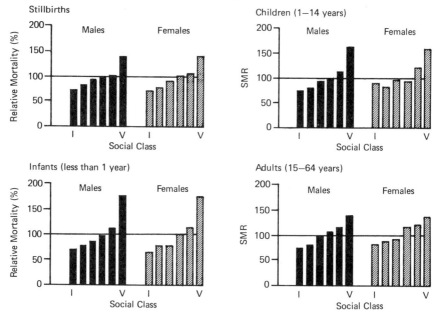

Source: *Occupational Mortality: 1970-72*(HMSO, London 1978). Reproduced with the permission of the Controller of Her Majesty's Stationery Office.

In figure 4.1 the incidence of mortality is represented by the standardised mortality ratio (SMR) which is a measure of the extent to which the mortality rate of each social class deviates from the average (100) of the age group as a whole. How much inequality in health in total is represented by this continuing pattern of class differentials in mortality risk from birth to retirement? One way of answering this question is to compare the life expectation of infants born to parents in social classes I and V respectively assuming that they remain throughout their working lives in the same social class. Proceeding in this way we would find a life expectation for a male infant in social class I of 72.19 years compared to 65.02 years for his counterpart in social class V. Thus a professional man's son is likely to live 7 years longer than the son of an unskilled worker.

Is the Gap in Life Chances between the Classes Increasing?

In chapter 2 we saw the way in which the general decline in mortality was associated with an increase of inequality in life chances between men and women. Now we must ask whether the same trends are found between the social classes. Answering this question involves the comparison of class gradients in mortality over time.

The study of trends in health inequality is complicated by shifts in the occupational structure during the course of this century which have led to a reduction in the percentage of the workforce in semi- and unskilled manual work and an expansion in non-manual jobs. A further complication is introduced by modifications that have been made to the RG scale which means that some occupations have been moved from one class to another thereby invalidating the practice of making comparisons between classes over time. For these reasons, questions about trends in the extent of health inequality can only be answered for the period since 1950 shortly after the introduction of the National Health Service. In the period since 1950, fewer changes have been made to the RG scale and those that have, can be offset by grouping together the adjacent classes between which most classificatory swops have been made. The period since 1960 is particularly instructive since this is one in which no changes were introduced.

Figure 4.2

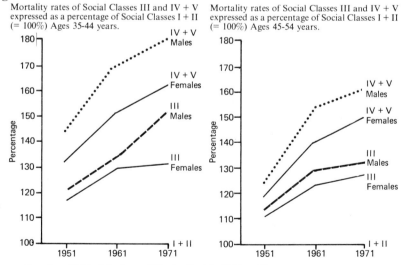

Mortality rates of Social Classes III and IV + V expressed as a percentage of Social Classes I + II (= 100%) Ages 35-44 years.

Mortality rates of Social Classes III and IV + V expressed as a percentage of Social Classes I + II (= 100%) Ages 45-54 years.

Source: Based on Table 3.3, *Inequalities in Health*, 1980, p.68.

In figure 4.2, social class I and II have been grouped together as have classes IV and V. The death rates for III and IV and V respectively have been expressed as a percentage excess of I and II. It can be seen immediately that, relative to social class I and II, the position of each of the other two grouped classes has deteriorated in each age group. On the basis of these data, the answer to the question 'Is health inequality becoming worse in England and Wales?' is yes.

Alternative Dimensions of Socio-Economic Inequality

The Registrar General's scale provides a means of approximating the extent of inequality between six broadly based occupational groups. In so doing it implies that the social and economic circumstances of the people who comprise each class are relatively homogeneous. But occupation is only one possible indicator of the distribution of power and resources stratifying life chances and we can safely assume that *within* occupational class, inequalities in health will also be found. Evidence of the kind of factors which produce variation within each class is found in the OPCS Longitudinal Survey. This survey, which is a sample of 1% of census returns linked to the system of death registration, provides a record of the census characteristics of people dying. From this source the relationship between education, region of residence, employment status, occupation and housing tenure with the risk of death in any age group can be examined.

Housing tenure provides a useful tool for exploring the extent of variation in health within each class. This is because it represents other aspects of socio-economic status. Apart from home ownership, it also stands for all the factors which enable people to acquire and maintain their own homes, including inheritance of property, stability of employment and income and credit-worthiness with the building societies. It is not surprising therefore that tenure proves to be a powerful tool for discriminating life chances *within* each occupational class. As figure 4.3 reveals, within each social class, the mortality of owner occupiers is substantially below that of people who rent their homes. Indeed there is more variation *between* owner occupiers and council tenants than there is between the social class divisions among home owners. This serves as a striking reminder that social and economic well-being can be measured in a number of ways and that any single variable like education chosen to indicate the extent of inequality provides only a partial guide to the full picture.

Another variable which performs the task of differentiating life chances within any of the six occupational classes is sex. In all age

Figure 4.3 Social Class, Tenure and Mortality, 1970-1975 (males aged 15-64)

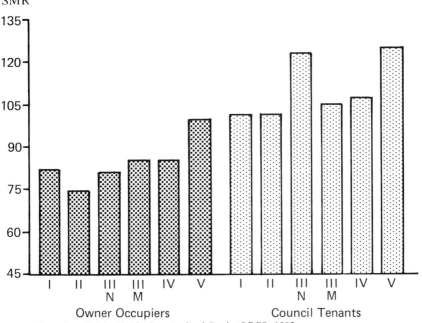

Owner Occupiers   Council Tenants

Source: Based on Table 13.5 in *Longitudinal Study*, OPCS, 1982.

groups, the risk of premature death for men is in excess of that for women. This is not revealed in figure 4.1 because the SMR has been calculated for men and women separately. When actual death rates within each sex and age group are compared directly, as they are in table 4.1, the full extent of sex inequality is revealed.

The following table shows two forms of inequality in health: occupational class and gender. For both sexes there are two and a half deaths among unskilled manual workers (V) for every one in the professional class (I). At the same time male death rates are almost double those of females in every class. This is indicated by the sex ratios for each class in column C. Indeed, apart from social class I, male death rates in every social class are consistently above even the highest rate recorded by women in social class V. The sex differential in mortality risk tends to increase with age whereas class differences become less significant as people get older. Among pre-school children, sex differences are somewhat less evident, but they become more marked as children grow into adolescence and adulthood (see figure 2.4 p.28).

Table 4.1   Death rates by sex and social class

Social Class	(A) Males	(B) Females	(C) Ratio Male to Female
I	3.98	2.15	1.85
II	5.54	2.85	1.94
IIIN	5.80	2.76	1.96
IIIM	6.08	3.41	1.78
IV	7.96	4.27	1.87
V	9.88	5.31	1.86
	2.5	2.5	

Source: Adapted from *Occupational Mortality 1970-72*
Females = Married women classified by their husbands occupation. Death rates per 1000 population

Sex and Class Differences in Mortality and Morbidity

Should we conclude from the foregoing picture of sex differences in mortality, that women are healthier than men? Certainly, if mortality is our measure there is little doubt that men are the disadvantaged sex. But when we examine other evidence of sickness and ill-health, a rather more complicated picture of sex-based health inequality emerges. This alternative indicator of health status is conventionally known as *morbidity*. It is usually measured through self reports of sickness and through records of medical consultation and treatment. Neither form of measure is entirely satisfactory. The former depends on individual judgement and action, while the latter besides being influenced by these subjective processes is also dependent on the supply of facilities for medical consultation and treatment. Neither type of measure can therefore be assumed to represent either a full or a standardised record of the extent of sickness in a population.

The reasons for adopting mortality to measure health were given in chapter 1 (p.3). Mortality is a more objective indicator of health status, it is easier to interpret and to apply to the analysis of trends in health over time. But is mortality a good substitute for morbidity including the subjective experience of ill-health sickness and disease? A comparison of the two among men and women, suggests that the answer to this question is no. Those whose lives are most likely to be prematurely brought to an end (i.e. men) do not seem to *experience* as much ill-health as those who live longer (i.e. women).

The following table compares sex and age differences in self reported morbidity and medical consultation from the General Household Survey (GHS) with mortality. For simplicity, the data are expressed in the form of ratios. Any figure above 1 means an excess of male morbidity or mortality and vice versa. By comparing the ratios in columns A to D with E, it is possible to see the extent to which the various measures of morbidity correlate with the relative risk of mortality. Thus, for example, among pre-school children, mortality rates are 34% higher among males but this greater vulnerability is not reflected in medical consultation where there is a slight female excess. The gap between the different types of health status indicator is at its widest between the ages of 65 and 74 where the mortality risk among men is almost double even though women make more frequent use of medical services.

Table 4.2   Sex Ratios in Self Reported Sickness, GP Consultation and Mortality
(Females = 1)

Age	(A) Consultation	(B) Chronic Illness	(C) Chronic Handicapping Illness	(D) Acute Illness	(E) Mortality
0-4	.97	1.13	1.5	1.13	1.34
5-14	1.01	1.38	1.67	1.10	1.36
15-44	.56	1.01	1.01	.92	1.67
45-64	1.01	1.05	1.13	1.00	1.83
65-74	.83	.91	.88	.74	1.93
75+	.99	.86	.90	.79	1.35

Source: Adapted from *General Household Survey 1974*
England and Wales

The tendency for mortality ratios to substantially exceed self reported morbidity is encountered in every age group over the age of 14. So it appears that although men consistently outnumber women in the risk of premature death, their vulnerability is not reflected in self reports of symptoms and medical consultation. While men die early, women suffer more sickness. Why should this be so? Is it because women are more vigilant about possible threats to their health, a fact reflected in their tendency to notice symptoms and resort to medical treatment? It seems doubtful that this could explain their lower mortality rates, since there is no effective therapy for most of the diseases which account for excess male mortality before retirement age. How else might we explain these sex differences in experience, behaviour and survival?

We have already considered some of the possible reasons for the increasing survival of women in the twentieth century in chapter 2 (pp.27-8). There we concluded that a persuasive reason for the dramatic divergence between male and female mortality rates since 1900 was found in the changing pattern of male and female domestic and occupational roles. These changes which have tended to make women more dependent both as housewives and clients of the welfare state, may also provide some clues to sex differences in mortality and morbidity.

It is possible that the phenomenon of morbidity in its various forms reflects a much broader range of social circumstances and experience than merely the symptoms of organic disorder that doctors treat? It is well known for example, that women are more likely to consult general practitioners about emotional, psychological, social and economic problems even though doctors feel ill-equipped to deal with them. Why are men more selective in their reasons for seeking medical advice? Is their need less because they experience greater autonomy over everyday life through work and the wage packet? If so, the gap between mortality and morbidity no longer seems paradoxical since the two measures reflect different dimensions of social inequality.

Inequalities in Health Care

The National Health Service (NHS) in Britain was established in 1948 by the post-war Labour government to provide a comprehensive system of health care with free access to everyone irrespective of the ability to pay. The implicit aim was to bring about equality of health in the population by making health care free. In its first thirty years the NHS has clearly not achieved this aim. Inequalities in health have persisted and worsened in the post-war period. There is nothing particularly surprising about this. As chapters 1 and 2 make clear, health is not determined by medical resources, it is the product of social and economic welfare. As long as inequalities of property, income, education, occupation and social privilege persist in a society, so will inequalities in health. The continuing picture of inequality in health in Britain is therefore like a barometer of socio-economic inequality in general.

Interestingly enough the NHS is also something of a barometer of the extent of inequality in the wider society. Despite the aim of its founders, the distribution of resources in the NHS is so unequal that one observer concluded it conformed to 'An Inverse Care Law' (Tudor-Hart, 1971). This law states that health care resources tend to be distributed in inverse proportion to need or put more simply, that those whose need is less get more resources, while those in greatest need get less. In practice this means that poor working class communities tend to have the shabbiest and most over-crowded facilities in the NHS. This happens because general practitioners prefer to work in more prosperous communities and consequently those who serve the poor have larger numbers of patients and less time for each consultation. The result is that the better off, whose need for health care is less, get a better deal out the NHS than the poor who have the highest rates of mortality and morbidity combined with a poorer standard of service.

How are these differences expressed in doctor/patient relation-ships? Studies of consulting room behaviour reveal that doctors spend more time with their middle class patients even within the same practice. Cartwright and O'Brian found that, while the average consultation with a middle class patient took 6.2 minutes, the working class equivalent took only 4.7 minutes. This time difference helps explain another finding that middle class patients get more information from their doctors, ask more questions and prove less easily satisfied with advice or treatment. And this was not all. Even though working class patients had been with the doctor for an average of 4 years longer, they were less well known. General practitioners had a better knowledge of their middle class patients and they were more likely to recognise them by name. This study suggests that medical consultation varies according to the social class of the patient. Treatment for the middle class appears to be more patient-centred (see p.104), focused on the needs of the consulter, while in the working class, it tends to be more doctor-centred, geared to the needs of the doctor. This may be the result of differences between patients. Middle class patients are probably more articulate and confident in reporting symptoms, and if they get better treatment, perhaps it is because they demand it. Could this also explain a further finding of Cartwright and O'Brian that, despite the fact that doctors have 'less sympathetic and understanding relationships with their working class patients', their consultations with them tend to be more satisfying?

> Our analyses show that doctors seemed to be more satisfied with consultations at which the conversation time was less than five minutes, where the patient asked not more than one question, and also possibly those at which fewer problems were discussed. (Cartwright and O'Brian 1974, 92).

Inequalities of treatment at the level of verbal exchange are probably equally prevalent when patients meet specialists in hospital, but it is not clear whether they influence the outcome of treatment. There are few up to date statistics available to study class differences in the benefit derived from hospital treatment. Cancer registration data suggest that middle class patients have better survival prospects, but this is probably the result of social class itself rather than anything encountered in treatment. One of the few studies that attempted to follow up patients discharged from a district general hospital, found marked differences in rates of survival by social class. Two years after discharge, less than 50% of patients could be described as 'cured' or improved of whom the majority were in non-manual occupations. The authors conclude:

> The transition from the sheltered atmosphere of the modern hospital ward to the icy chill of the workaday world, is indeed a testing time and it is not surprising that many soon break down. The ex-patients who showed the heaviest mortality at early ages, the strongest tendency to relapse and the poorest record in point of early return to work, were the group of unskilled labourers . . . In many cases early recurrence of breakdown came from bad social conditions rather than any inevitability on medical grounds. (Ferguson and McPhail 1954, 137).

It is obvious that the NHS cannot compensate for the structure of social and economic inequality in the community at large. But has it even tried?

In 1976 the government adopted the recommendations of a report on the reallocation of resources in the NHS. The 'RAWP' report recommended that there should be a redistribution of the NHS budget to areas which had never received a fair share of available resources. These areas included some with the highest mortality rates in Britain. The report showed that the areas best endowed with health service facilities had the lowest mortality rates. Even so these areas in south-east England had been allocated a much larger than average per capita share of the NHS budget every year since 1948. Table 4.3, summarises the lack of fit between indicators of need for health care (infant and adult mortality rates) and the distribution of health care resources.

Table 4.3   Regional Inequalities in Health and Health Care in the UK, 1977

Region	Mortality			NHS Expenditure		
	Males	Females	Infants	Hospitals	GPs	Nurses
ENGLAND	99	99	13.7	61.76	4.84	73.5
Northern	111	109	14.9	56.19	4.55	71.4
Yorkshire	105	105	15.5	56.86	4.70	73.6
Trent	103	102	13.9	50.9	4.54	66.1
East Anglia	89	96	11.2	53.83	4.85	65.6
NW Thames	89	90	11.8	74.91	5.48	75.4
NE Thames	94	92	14.0	76.35	5.10	76.6
SE Thames	95	92	13.1	73.61	5.01	80.5
SW Thames	90	95	11.6	67.00	5.17	76.5
Wessex	92	92	13.1	52.44	4.98	68.5
Oxford	90	96	12.7	53.18	4.73	62.3
South Western	93	97	12.5	57.58	5.17	74.7
West Midlands	103	103	15.0	52.65	4.56	67.9
Mersey	110	109	14.4	62.16	4.60	80.6
North Western	113	111	14.8	57.63	4.55	75.0
WALES	108	106	13.5	61.50	5.05	79.0
SCOTLAND	112	109	16.1	78.10	5.98	102.2
N. IRELAND	112	115	17.2	83.07	4.98	77.1

Source: Adapted from *The Report of the Royal Commission on the National Health Service*, 1980 (Tables 3.1, 3.2 & 3.3). GPs and Nurses per 10,000 population. Hospital Expenditure = £ per capita. Mortality = SMRs for males and females. Infant mortality per 1000 live births.

This inequality is a built-in feature of the NHS. It results from the tendency to allocate resources on the basis of what already exists rather than on the basis of need in a fundamental sense. The technical word for it is incrementalism. The principal reason for the continued overfunding of the richest parts of the country at the expense of the poorest, was simply that most of the prestigious teaching hospitals are in London and these absorbed a large and, in the past, generally unquestioned share of available resources. As a result people at greater health risk in heavily industrialised parts of the country had worse medical facilities than their fellow citizens in London and the home counties. It is unlikely that this would explain the reasons for unequal mortality risk. Most premature death is incurable and as table 4.3 shows there is no correlation between mortality risk and share of the NHS budget. The healthiest part of Britain, East Anglia, has never received a fair share, while Scotland, with the worst record of health, gets 50% more per head of population that England and Wales as a whole.

Since the implementation of RAWP, a process of reallocating the NHS budget has been underway. Coming at the same time as public expenditure cuts, it has led to the closure or threatened closure of a large number of hospitals in London. One unfortunate result has probably been to make access to medical care in poor inner city areas even worse. The prevalence of 'shut-up shop' style general practices manned by deputising services out of hours made the local hospital the best hope of emergency treatment for many people. Their closure will mean that the cost of any redistribution that takes place from London to the rest of the country will be born by the poor rather than the better off.

The evidence in table 4.3 also serves to illustrate another dimension of health inequality to contemporary Britain. This is inequality based on region. People resident in the north of England, Scotland, Wales and Northern Ireland live shorter lives. Regional differences have been evident ever since statistics were kept. It used to be thought that they were no more than an expression of occupational class, since areas of high mortality have a larger preponderance of manual workers whose average mortality would tend to be higher. However this is not the case. Controlling for the class composition of each region makes very little difference to mortality risk. What this means is that death rates within each class are lower in London or Brighton than they are in Manchester or Sheffield. The exact causes of regional inequalities remain obscure.

Explaining Class Inequalities in Health

Class inequalities in health have been accounted for in a number of different ways. The report of the DHSS *Inequalities in Health Working Group* ('The Black Report'), lists four types of explanation. These are:- (1) Inequality as an artefact; (2) Inequality as natural selection; (3) Inequality as material deprivation; (4) Inequality as cultural deprivation. How does each account for the evidence of health inequality surveyed above?

(a) Health inequality as an artefact

The artefact explanation argues that inequalities in health are not real but artificial. They are an *effect* produced in the attempt to measure something which is more complicated than the tools of measurement can appreciate. More an expression of scepticism than a theoretical explanation, this view is held by statisticians who claim that the evidence of health inequality is so complicated by changes of classification etc. that it is impossible to tell whether things are getting better or worse. Furthermore it is argued that changes in the occupational structure are likely to combine with age to confound *any* attempt to measure inequality in mortality even at one point in time. It is suggested that the age structure of social class V is likely to be biased towards older workers because younger recruits to the labour force will have entered better paid, more skilled occupations, that have expanded since the war. Since mortality risk increases with the age, this effect is likely to enlarge the rate of social class V as a whole. If so, the observed gradient is really caused by the skewed age structure of the unskilled manual class rather than by the poorer health of its members. Age specific mortality differences cast doubt on the validity of this explanation for they show that inequality tends to reduce with age and that it is among younger people that inequality is most pronounced and moreover increasing. (See figure 4.2). This means that the evidence of inequality in mortality risk is not an artefact, but a real phenomenon of class advantage and disadvantage which must be explained in other ways.

(b) Health inequality as a selection process

The most persuasive attempt to explain health inequalities as the outcome of a process natural selection, has been put forward by the statistician, Jon Stern. He argues that observed inequalities in mortality between socio-economic groups like the Registrar General's social classes, reflect a process of social mobility in which individuals with better health move up the social hierarchy, while those in poorer health move down. Paradoxically this exchange of people up and down the socio-economic hierarchy, reflecting as it does an open class structure, creates an effect of worsening inequality in measured differentials. His argument can be illustrated by way of a hypothetical example. Let us assume two social classes which we will simply call the rich and the poor. Stern argues that the exchange of people between these classes will take the form of upward mobility on the part of the healthy poor and downward mobility on the part of the unhealthy rich. This means that the rich class sheds its unhealthy members and gains new healthy recruits from the poor, while the poor lose their most healthy people and get as replacements people who cannot hold on to their wealth because of poor health. The overall result of this two-way exchange is to improve measurements of *average* health status among the rich while depressing those of the poor. Social mobility therefore reinforces any health inequality in this imaginary two class society by widening the gap in survival chances between rich and poor. This leads Stern to conclude that the measurement of change in class gradients in health should be conducted on the basis of class of origin rather than achieved social class. This is a good example of an important *methodological* problem in sociological research. The survey method, the sociologist's primary instrument for gathering data produces a vision of the individual as a snapshot, a collection of social attributes at one point in time. This has the effect of disguising the historical dimension of every human lifetime and variation in personal experience over time is lost to sociological view.

To support his argument, Stern draws on the research of Illsley (1950) which linked the upward and downward mobility of women at marriage to their health status and intelligence. Illsley concluded that the lower infant mortality of higher social classes was the result of better maternal health indicated by such factors as the height of women. Of particular interest was the fact that women from lower social classes who had been upwardly mobile, were very healthy and their inclusion in the higher class improved its average as a whole. From this evidence Stern is led to conclude that observed class differences in health, far from showing that trends in social and economic deprivation are worsening, are actually compatible with greater fluidity in the class structure and hence greater opportunity in society. As he argues, if social mobility were more difficult or even impossible as in a caste system, inequalities in health would disappear since the poor would retain those in good health and the rich those in bad health thereby maintaining parity in average health status.

In effect Stern defines health as a fixed or genetic property of individuals largely independent of their immediate social and economic circumstances. This view is contrary to a sociological account which sees health as primarily a product of the social and economic environment. His argument rests on the assumption that health itself increases the probability of social mobility and that the class structure permits movement up and down. This means that no matter how deprived the social background, a genetic potentiality for good health will enable a person to overcome material disadvantage and 'climb out' of poverty. To prove or disprove this thesis would require data which trace the progress of individuals throughout the course of their lives. Since most sociological and statistical data lack this biographical dimension, it is impossible to settle the claims of this thesis one way or the other. Its plausibility depends on the extent to which people can insulate their health from material disadvantage during the course of their lifetimes. This leads to a consideration of the importance of material deprivation in shaping health and survival prospects.

(c) Health inequality as material deprivation

Material deprivation means a shortage of the material resources on which healthy human existence depends. In less developed societies its effects may appear in very high death rates from diseases primarily caused by malnutrition and exposure. The poorest sections of the community simply lack adequate resources to maintain the material substance of their bodies or to protect them from the natural environment. In this form, material deprivation may be accepted as a fact of life only surfacing to remind the better off that it is the result of material inequality when deaths from starvation-related disease occur in epidemic proportions. In earlier centuries in our own society, massive mortality from 'pestilence' occurred frequently against the background of war and bad harvest. The heaviest toll of death was amongst the poor, whose inadequate nutritional state made them the easiest targets for infective organisms (see p.31). In modern times death on this scale is only encountered in the Third World and then not often on the scale of the Ethiopian 'Human Tragedy'.

Where material deprivation has an immediate, visible impact, it seems to constitute an absolute shortage of essential needs. One might imagine a dividing line of economic welfare called basic subsistence below which human survival is put at risk. However in practice it is not possible to define a minimum subsistence level in this way because rates of human survival are not fixed. When living standards rise, both rich and poor improve their life expectation and the gap in life chances is maintained. But if life expectation can be extended even for the poorest members of the community, then there can be no *absolute* standard of subsistence that ensures good health. The definition of deprivation is always relative to social and economic norms. In these terms inequality in survival rates between the social classes is the product of fundamental inequalities in the distribution of wealth and income. This was the explanation favoured by the DHSS chief scientist and other members of the Working Group on Inequalities in Health.

Table 4.4   Social Class, Average Weekly Income and Standardised Mortality Ratios

Social Class	Average Weekly Income (£s)	SMR
I	44.14	77
II	34.02	81
IIIN (non-manual)	24.12	99
IIIM (manual)	27.05	106
IV	22.46	114
V	22.09	137

Source: Adapted from *Occupational Mortality 1970-72*, p. 151
       (men aged 15-64)

Table 4.4 displays the relationship between mortality risk and one dimension of material deprivation, inequalities in weekly income.

Average weekly income is closely related to the risk of dying before retirement. Only among clerical workers (IIIN) is the gradient disturbed. Their average income is below that of IIIM, yet their SMR is lower.. Apart from the incorporation of overtime earnings in the average for IIIM, this divergence is likely to reflect the greater safety of the work environment of social class IIIN and the relative youth of non-manual workers. Among men, social class IIIN tends to be a transient phase in the career, a mid-point on the way up the occupational ladder. This is generally not the case among skilled manual workers for whom IIIM is lifetime class location. This serves as a reminder that income is only one dimension of occupational class. Other dimensions include prospects for personal development and the nature of the work people carry out in order to earn their livelihood. The greater hazards of manual work are reflected in the risk of accidents at work. (Figure 4.4). In sociological terms this means that, in their contribution to the *Social Division of Labour,* manual workers must systematically expose their health to greater risk.

Figure 4.4 Mortality by Social Class for Accidents at Work (men aged 15-64)

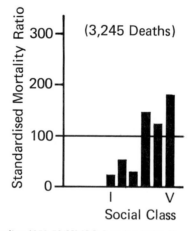

Source: *Occupational Mortality: 1970-72*(HMSO, London 1978). Reproduced with the permission of the Controller of Her Majesty's Stationery Office.

Income and work conditions are two possible indicators of material welfare and deprivation in contemporary Britain. Other important dimensions include: being employed or unemployed, security of tenure in employment, job satisfaction, expectation for retirement pension and not least important, the possession of wealth and property itself. We have seen some of these factors at work producing variation in mortality risk according to house ownership (p.55). Another dimension also of relevance is ownership of society's productive system: the land, large corporations and firms, factories, banks, insurance companies, even the means of communication themselves, newspapers and commercial television companies. How might this form of private wealth ownership, literally of Britain's economy itself, play a part in determining the distribution of life chances in society?

In Britain the ownership of private wealth is highly concentrated in a relatively small sector of the community. In 1972, according to the Royal Commission on the Distribution of Income and Wealth, 89% of the private wealth ownership was in the hands of 20% of the population. Within this group, the richest 1%, 5% and 10% respectively owned 30%, 56% and 72% of wealth accounted for in Inland Revenue returns. This highly unequal concentration of property ownership is, in Marxist theory, *the axis* of class stratification in capitalist society. It gives rise to two classes: those who own the means of production and those who are propertyless. The owners, the capitalist class, run the national economy in their own interests according to the rules of profit and loss. Profits are generated through the accumulation of surplus value. This is the value produced in the labour process after costs including wages have been deducted. Capitalism is an exploitative economic system according to Marx, because workers are alienated from what they produce and because they do not receive its full value as wages. In the middle of the nineteenth century, when Marx was developing his theories, the working class was, by any standard, terribly exploited. The working week was seven days and the working day was ten hours long. The employment of small children in mines and factories, which is illegal today, was commonplace. It was against this background that Marx identified the processes of *immiserisation* and *polarisation*, integral features of the capitalism of his day. They are manifested in the drive for profit which leads to a lowering of wages and to a worsening of work conditions finally leaving the worker with insufficient resources to maintain bodily health or, as Marx put it, 'to reproduce his labour power'. The fall in wages and living standards affects the whole workforce with the result that *all* workers become more impoverished. This has a unifying effect. It leads to the polarisation of owners and workers into two distinct classes with opposed economic interests.

The advent of Keynesian economics cast these processes in a rather different light. Keynes argued that economic growth and the profitability of firms depends primarily on the level of consumer spending. In this light forcing down wages is a shortsighted route to capital accumulation since it has a negative effect on the economy as a whole. Keynes provided a rationale for government intervention in the management of the economy to regulate the supply of money and maintain high levels of demand in order to protect firms and their employees from the periodic cycle of boom and recession. From a Keynesian perspective it is not so clear that the interests of workers and owners are fundamentally opposed and in the post-war era the adoption of Keynesian policies has brought about substantial improvements in living standards.

In consequence the population has not been polarised in the way Marx predicted. As the evidence presented earlier testifies, it is more instructive to see the structure of inequality as a stratified hierarchy rather than a two class division. For this reason, the concepts of immiserisation and polarisation appear irrelevant to the circumstances of modern capitalism. This is why modern Marxists refer to relative as opposed to absolute exploitation (see p.39). The modern mode of exploitation is to foist unnecessary commodities on people creating a materialistic society where things become more important than human relationships. The drive to consumption leads people to make money and work their main priority, which in turn undermines the social relationships which make life meaningful and worthwhile. In general the statistical evidence of health inequality suggests that poverty, defined relative to prevailing living standards, is more closely correlated to premature death than is the accumulation of modern commodities. This seems paradoxical because as we saw in chapter 2, infective diseases caused by poverty and malnutrition have been replaced by degenerative diseases associated with smoking, rich diet and inactivity. In these changed circumstances, the idea of health inequality being due to material shortage seems less persuasive. This is why some observers have been persuaded by the idea that cultural divisions between the classes determine health and survival. In what follows the scope of cultural deprivation as an explanation for health inequality will be explored and further consideration will be given to the role of poverty as a source of ill-health in contemporary society in chapter 5 (p.93).

(d) Health inequality as cultural deprivation

Part of the culture of any social group is concerned with ideas and practices about health. In earlier centuries it was believed that sickness and disease were the product of supernatural causes, the work of either

God or the Devil. The medieval man of God doubled as healer and monasteries were also pharmacies. As medical treatment was on balance rather dangerous, faith healing with its potential *placebo* effect, probably offered the most effective response to sickness. The incorporation of healing within religion therefore had a certain rationality. With the development of science and technology in the wake of industrialisation, these cultural beliefs about the impotence of human intervention in matters of health were gradually swept away. It took a long time. The history of the incorporation of contraception, abortion and artificial insemination as acceptable cultural practice, is an interesting, topical case study of the continuing hold of religious morality over the rights of human intervention in bodily processes. Today there is little doubt that contemporary cultural beliefs about health and disease have been captured by medicine. We shall have more to say about the culture of modern medicine and its role in present day society in chapters 6 and 7.

The culture of an advanced industrial society is heavily influenced by science and technology and by universal literacy. It is moreover much less stable than the systems of belief of earlier times. By its very nature, it is subject to a continuous process of reappraisal and modification; it reaches out and communicates with larger and larger populations through media of its own creation. Advanced technological media such as the television, the computer, or the intercontinental communication satellite are examples. The script of modern culture therefore requires individuals to be flexible. Nothing is fixed, knowledge and skill are continually on the move and individuals must be prepared to adapt their ideas, behaviour and relationships to keep up. The resulting instability is offset by advanced forms of communication such as the telephone, the television and the motor car, basic possessions of the average household. They allow individuals to get in touch with people easily and rapidly, to keep up to date with what's new, and to move about at will. In this way modern men and women are able to experience a sense, at least, of control over their immediate circumstances. This, in part, is what is meant by an individualistic way of life.

These tendencies of modern culture are beginning to be expressed in beliefs about the causes of disease. The major causes of death today are increasingly thought of as the outcome of degenerative processes, of human bodies literally wearing out. Given that nobody lives forever, this must happen to everyone sometime in their lives. But, the message goes, people should be capable of regulating the life of bodies in some degree, by looking after them properly. The scope for personal health care includes diet, exercise, the effective use of medical services and the avoidance of bad habits like smoking. In this way the life of organs like the heart, can be prolonged and the onset of disease prevented or rather put off. Naturally, people who do not heed the advice, are likely to die earlier.

The need to teach the public how to look after itself, has given rise to a new profession. The ethos of health education work is that the secret of good health lies in the hands of individuals themselves. This leads to a tendency to locate the causes of premature death at the same door. Lower class people therefore are sometimes seen as the victims of their own cultural backwardness, being either ignorant of good health practice or too inert to do anything about it. This was how Brotherston (1976) explained the greater mortality of babies in social class V households — their mothers came too late for ante-natal care. He drew this conclusion in the absence of evidence proving that ante-natal care made any difference to the survival prospects of infants. Since then research has questioned its value by showing that it is not effective at identifying mothers and babies at risk *(Hall et al* 1980). Nevertheless, to Brotherston, the problem seemed to be one of lower class women clinging to their own culture of childbirth and resisting, and therefore losing out on, the benefits of medical technology.

If this situation is one of cultural deprivation, then the source of the problem should be located not in the individual but in the failure of new cultural practices to penetrate the lives of lower class people. Culture is a concept which embraces a collectivity, it is the ideas and practices of a *group* and to survive, it must be interwoven in the beliefs of a community. This was how Oscar Lewis employed the concept to describe the mechanisms which perpetuated poverty in the Mexican families he wrote about. His *Culture of Poverty* consisted of the ideas, behaviours and strategies, poor people adopt in order to cope with the perpetual material deprivations of their lives. Their methods of surviving in a harsh environment, by infiltrating their culture, take on a life of their own. As a result, they are likely to persist even if the economic environment changes for the better. This leads to the Community being imprisoned in poverty by its beliefs and its habitual behaviour. This is what constitutes *cultural deprivation.*

Can this explain the excess mortality of the working class? Could it be the product of outmoded and redundant cultural norms, the result not of their relationship to the means of production but to the shifting cultural norms of advanced capitalist societies? Let us explore the scope of this 'poverty of health culture' thesis with a concrete example.

Among causes which contribute to the higher mortality of manual workers, the most important is lung cancer. In 1970-72, this cause accounted for 40,000 deaths of men aged 15-64 years (40% of all cancer mortality in the age group). Although the aetiology of this disease remains poorly understood, it is well known that heavy smokers carry five times the risk of non-smokers. In the last 15 years smoking has become strongly class-related. In 1960, there was little difference between the social classes in the consumption of cigarettes. Since then, consumption in the middle class has fallen off substantially, leaving a class gradient in tobacco consumption which closely reflects the gradient for lung cancer mortality.

Figure 4.5

Cigarette consumption by Social Class (males aged 15-64).

Deaths from Lung Cancer by Social Class (males aged 15-64).

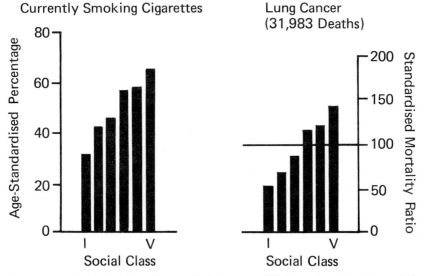

Source: *Occupational Mortality: 1970-72* (HMSO, London 1978). Reproduced with the permission of the Controller of Her Majesty's Stationery Office.

The general correspondence between these gradients implies that higher death rates are largely due to heavy smoking. This leads to the question why the people most at risk of premature death, have failed to take heed of the message that smoking is bad for your health. Could it be ignorance? Is it possible that manual workers have not understood the warning on each deadly packet? Since this is hardly likely to be the reason, we must look elsewhere for an explanation of this apparently dangerous class-related behaviour.

Remember that the behaviour in question is not a series of random individual acts. It is a group phenomenon, a cultural norm rather than a personal habit. This raises the possibility that the failure of health education to make the impact on manual workers as elsewhere in the population, is because smoking remains closely interwoven with the culture of everyday life. In the past, smoking has been a socially valued behaviour. It was deliberately encouraged in two world wars when cheap cigarettes became one of the perks of being in uniform. Among the young, smoking has long been a significant symbol of the transition from school to the labour market and from childhood to adult independence. Increasing consumption among women perhaps testifies to its continuing importance as a symbol of personal independence, of 'growing up' into adult (labour market) social roles. Giving up therefore involves more than overcoming what is in any case an addictive habit. It also requires a cultural redefinition of the behaviour. Why should this be more difficult in working as opposed to middle class circles? It is easy to see how a declining rate of smoking would serve to reinforce a negative sanction against the behaviour and vice versa. As smoking becomes a culturally despised habit among the middle classes, those who persist become exposed to group pressures to give up. Meanwhile continued high consumption among manual workers positively reinforces and perpetuates the habit. But how does the cultural redefinition of smoking begin and flourish in one section of society and not in another?

It must be said that the cultural 'recoding' of smoking, a pleasurable habit, will be more easily achieved if there are substitutes to satisfy the physical and cultural needs it fulfills. This may require for example the identification of other symbols of impending adult status to denote social independence. Manual workers make the transition from school to work earlier, when they are still quite young. This may be why they have more need of external symbols of the status change. Middle class lives are in any case less uniform and the transition is less likely to be a one-off but a continuing development involving further education or training and occupational career developments. No wonder then, that the symbolic value of smoking is less. What of the physical needs that smoking satisfies? Here we must ask whether the seeming reluctance of manual workers to take the health warning seriously, is because of its narcotic value as a means of reducing the sheer physical stress of manual work. If so the problem is one of material not cultural deprivation. On the other hand if smoking is not a pacifying drug but is really just a pleasurable activity, then giving up may simply denote the availability of a wider range of other sources of enjoyment.

Another possibility is that middle class men and women have responded more rapidly to the idea that smoking is bad for your health because their socialisation leaves them better equipped to adapt to the shifting character of modern culture. Group solidarity is less important in their lives because they experience more social and geographical mobility. Individualism is not merely an ideological banner, they have direct experience of it in their personal lives in the absence of any lasting attachment to particular groups or communities. Consequently the redefinition of a cultural norm in terms of everyday behaviour may gather momentum more rapidly because it depends more on individual initiative. Furthermore behavioural innovation, in this more privatised world, is less subject to negative group sanctions.

Giving up cigarettes is a form of deferred gratification, a valued social activity is sacrificed in order to reap some future benefit. As with all preventive health care measures nobody can be completely sure that the sacrifice will pay off. Like the Calvinist entrepreneurs who inspired Max Weber, one only discovers if one is among the elect at the end of the road and the best insurance meanwhile, is to act as if one were. Preventive strategies, in the absence of hard evidence stem from hope and conviction, but they still imply that the individual possesses some sense that the course of life is something over which a degree of control may be exerted. This sense of 'self mastery' over personal circumstances is also a more prevalent middle class expectation.

This fits with research findings from the United States linking class differences in ageing to outmoded cultural norms. Blue collar workers are said to *feel* old at a younger chronological age than white collar age peers. Because white collar workers expect to survive to a healthy old age, they take steps in advance to preserve their looks and their bodies. The more limited survival horizons of blue collar workers, on the other hand, leads to a fatalistic approach to the ageing of the body. They literally 'let themselves go' to an early grave. This suggests that people who try to become the architects of their own health by regulating consumption, by jogging etc., can actually influence their life expectation. This portrayal of a person's *sense* of being in control, as an important factor in the ageing process might be called a *poverty of health culture thesis.*

The problem with research like this however is that it is very difficult to determine whether subjective individual assessments of health actually reflect the *material* realities of growing old. Perhaps the *sense* that nothing can be done to slow down the 'clock of life' is a rational response to poverty and powerlessness. Equally, the expectation that the future is within personal control may arise because to some extent it is among those who possess a larger share of power and resources to plan their lives. A sense of self mastery in these terms is not so much a product of the imagination as one of pension rights, bank balance and property ownership. At this point, cultural deprivation shades into a material form and leaves open the question of how useful the distinction between the cultural and material dimensions of life is to the analysis of social inequality.

Health Inequality: Questions and Answers

The explanations for health inequality, discussed in the last section, differ in their assumptions, their conclusions and in the way that questions are posed. Artefact explanations tend to be favoured by statisticians and by sociologists who reject statistical data altogether on the familiar grounds that 'There are lies, damn lies and statistics'. It is not a theoretical explanation on a par with the other three. It consists of a set of negative conclusions emerging from attempts to test theory with available data: the data are not adequate for the task of theoretical evaluation. This conclusion can be expressed with a number of different emphases which have different implications. On the one hand it might be concluded that *There is no evidence of health inequality in present day Britain.* On the other, it could be said that *The available statistics leave the question unsettled one way or the other.*

It might be thought unfortunate that difficulties of interpretation makes the task of choosing between competing theories well nye impossible. In practice, however, in both medicine and social science, it is very often the case that empirical data leave plenty of room for controversy. Research findings can all too often be stretched to support a number of even opposed theoretical explanations. In consequence theoretical evaluation usually turns out to be a rather complicated task requiring judgements about the structure of a theoretical argument including its assumptions as well as the fit with empirical proof. As we have seen (p.53), despite problems of reclassification etc., the statistics of class-related mortality give grounds to believe that during the post-war era social class mortality gradients were still very much in evidence and more seriously so among younger age groups.

The other explanations identified by the Black Report have theoretical aims. Our attention has already been drawn to the fact that two of them are essentially sociological explanations and that the other is not. What difference does this make?

The argument that inequality in health reflects material or cultural deprivation is a sociological position. It states that health is the product of social forces whether these take a material (economic) or a cultural (normative) form. Health is *assumed* to be a property of the social environment and of the individual's relationship to it. In sociology therefore health is defined in *relational* terms. It is *relative* to place, time and class. At the same time inequality is also located as a property of structures and forces ultimately beyond individual characteristics and control. It also has a *relational* form. From this perspective, economic or cultural well-being has little to do with personal initiative, energy or skill, and everything to do with the inheritance of wealth, education and social privilege including their influence on socialisation. It is the individual's *relationship* to the distribution of these valued social resources that determines the socio-economic course of his or her lifetime. While some may escape from a poor social background up the ladder of social mobility, the structure or framework of class inequality persists from one generation to the next to determine the welfare of the majority who are left behind.

How does the other type of explanation differ from this? The alternative thesis, at its crudest level, traces inequalities in life expectation quite literally to the 'survival of the fittest'. Health is conceived as an integral property of individuals which enables them to escape from a low social class to a higher one. Indeed it implies that the whole hierarchy of social class is itself strongly influenced by the tendency of the 'fit' and the 'unfit' to exchange positions on the social ladder. Class differences therefore arise from the sum of the personal attributes of the people who occupy each rank and any social structure of inequality contained within social institutions, recedes into the background. A dominating feature of this approach therefore is the emphasis on the individual and the role of personal attributes in the process of social stratification be it health or wealth.

The ingredients for each type of explanation are therefore quite different. The explanatory problem is shaped in each case by a distinctive set of assumptions which in turn help to influence any conclusions reached. The natural selection thesis provides a plausible account of the mechanisms which may translate social mobility into a deceptive picture of health inequality. Its validity depends on the extent to which its key assumption, that health itself is an independent and determining factor in social mobility, is accepted. In the alternative approach, the problem to be explained is defined differently. With health now appearing as a dependent variable, a product of social and economic life, the question at issue is whether *the structure of inequality* is getting better or worse. It is taken for granted that the distribution of life chances in the population will reflect the level of inequality in society. As with the selection thesis, the validity of any conclusions depend upon the soundness of initial assumptions.

Proponents of most theories can usually find some modicum of empirical support for their favourite conclusions and for this reason it is seldom possible to choose between competing explanations on the grounds of evidence alone. Whether a theory is accepted or rejected has as much to do with whether the assumptions and hence the whole tenor of the argument are in tune with whoever is listening. The natural selection thesis starts with the advantage of a definition of health which fits well, with, is perhaps even drawn from contemporary medical practice. Doctors focus on the *socially anonymous individual,* the patient. Given that popular knowledge about health is generated through encounters with doctors, the assumption that it is a natural biological feature of individuals may be widely acceptable. Against this, in any careful analysis, must be weighed the historical evidence which shows that health status is highly sensitive to material living standards. This evidence reinforces the argument that correlations between income, property and the risk of death in the present day, follow the pattern of the past.

Is it either necessary or possible to choose between these types of explanation? Can the pattern of health inequality be the product of both processes acting together, so that the tendency for healthy people to improve their social status actually increases measured differentials which are already shaped in large degree by social class in its various dimensions. If this happens then it must mean that upward mobility on account of health occurs despite, even in the face of, socio-economic deprivation. But how can personal health be insulated for some people in a harsh environment but not for the majority? Or to put it another way, how does the genetic health potential of an individual, destined for social mobility, escape the systematic and continuous environmental processes that shape the experience of everyone else in the same community?

These crucial questions about the nature of health cannot be satisfactorily answered because of a lack of empirical evidence. They involve the investigation of individual life careers from birth to death, tracing all critical points of change in both socio-economic and health circumstances. General Practitioners are probably the best placed to accumulate the necessary evidence. But because they are socialised within the bio-mechanical model, they tend to favour more individuated explanations of health focusing on personal biology and psychology. The next chapter will introduce further evidence relating to sociological approaches to understanding how health develops through the course of life, in response to social and economic circumstances.

Chapter Five

Becoming Ill as a Social Process

The most obvious symptoms of disease in the human body are physiological in form. They are tangible biological phenomena — tumours, blood clots, burst arteries, kidney stones, congested lungs — and it is only natural to assume that they are caused by the same kind of organic material or that their formation is stimulated by biological processes. In this chapter we will examine the evidence for the claim that the roots of organic disease are to be found in social life itself, in personality, in behaviour, and in social relationships. By this account the physical manifestations of organic disorder, while real enough, are in effect no more than the end product of social and psychological experiences encountered in everyday life. In short, disease is a case of mind over matter.

Life Events and Illness

Does personal anxiety arising out of unhappy experiences in the course of the lifetime hold vital clues about the causes of organic disease? This line of theorising, although novel in scientific circles, is by no means new. The belief that worry leads to illness or even death is a longstanding tradition in our own society. Certainly in other cultures, the causes of sickness and disease are thought primarily to lie in troubled social relationships. The Azande of the Sudan studied by Evans-Pritchard, believe that organic illness is the result of witchcraft directed at the sufferer by some unknown person who 'wishes him ill'. Likewise among the Nuer, another Sudanese tribe, studied by the same anthropologist, sickness is liable to be explained by such events as sexual infidelity. These forms of belief are dismissed by Western science as being irrational and mystical. But there is evidence in our own advanced industrial civilisation, that personal crises prompted by disruptive social relationships lead to disease.

In a study published under the title of *Broken Heart,* Rees and Lutkins demonstrated that, in the year following the death of their wives, widowers were subject to an increased risk of dying themselves. When compared to a control group matched for age and occupation, newly widowed men were 40% more likely to die of a number of causes, the most frequent being heart disease. After the first year of bereavement the excess mortality of the widowers fell back to the level of the control group. The authors concluded that the stress of losing their wives was a serious risk factor for heart disease and that there might be some truth in the old belief that people die of a broken heart. The increased susceptibility of the widowed to heart attacks is well documented in other research as is their greater vulnerability to that other great killer of modern civilisation, cancer. Similar results have also been found for the divorced and separated suggesting that the loss of a marriage partner poses a particularly important threat to health.

This fact was noticed more than eighty years ago by the French sociologist Emile Durkheim, who pointed out that suicide rates were systematically linked to social variables like religion and marital status He insisted that this was a function of social integration. The lives of married people are more subject to normative regulation which strengthens the will to survive. The single and the formerly married on the other hand, lead a more 'anomic' existence which weakens it. This protective feature of being married is not restricted to the risk of suicide. As figure 5.1 reveals, the risks of premature death from *all* causes are closely correlated with marital status, suggesting that having a partner enhances survival prospects and that being without one exposes people to greater risks of all kinds. These data support Durkheim's contention that people bound together in supportive social relationships find everyday life more meaningful. Following him even further we could go on to argue that premature death is a social phenomenon, or as he would have put it a *Social Fact.*

Durkheim's interpretation of the correlation between marriage and the risk of suicide presents individual motivation as a socially constructed phenomenon. The individual's sense that life is worth living is not a matter of personal psychology, it is a reflection of the circumstances of married life, of moral regulation and mutual support. Anticipating the ideas to be examined in the next chapter, we could infer that marriage is a social role which involves a number of normative rights and duties. This creates a sense of obligation and belongingness which not only strengthens the individual's will to live, in a subjective sense, it actually appears to protect the very physical substance of their bodies.

Figure 5.1 Death Rates by Sex, Age and Marital Status

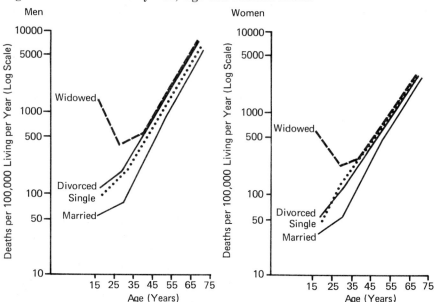

Source: *Occupational Mortality: 1970-72*(HMSO, London, 1978) Reproduced with the permission of the Conrtoller of Her Majesty's Stationery Office.

Meanwhile other research suggests that the loss of all kinds of important social relationships and valued social statuses increase the individual's susceptibility to a wide range of diseases. In his book, *The Social Causes of Illness* Totman reviews the evidence linking disruptive life events such as widowhood, separation, adultery, divorce, job change, unemployment, migration, retirement and eviction to a multitude of conditions including leukaemia, tuberculosis, pernicious anaemia, heart failure, asthma, multiple sclerosis, breast and cervical cancer and even the common cold. The array of evidence supporting this so-called *Loss/Disease Hypothesis* is impressive but most of it is surrounded by a methodological controversy. Many of the studies which report an association between life events and disease have been retrospective in design relying on the reconstructed reports of personal crises of people already suffering from a particular disease. Such evidence is of dubious validity for as Totman observes:

> Human memory, in particular, the memory of emotionally charged
> events, is not like a passive store. Its contents become distorted and
> elaborated with the passage of time. Thus when someone is asked by an

interviewer to recount past events which have distressed him, he cannot be relied upon to produce an 'objective commentary'. (Totman 1979, 113).

Attempts to overcome this methodological objection have led to the development of more objective methods for recording life events in the individual's past. One of these is the Holmes-Rahe Social Readjustment Rating Scale (the SRRS), a series of experiences involving the loss or rejection of a single social relationship, a set of relationships, or a valued part of the personal identity. This scale is made up of 42 events which are all held to require some degree of social adjustment when they happen to a person. The events are arranged hierarchically according to how they were scored by a sample of 400 healthy Americans who were asked to judge how much 'life change' each was likely to involve. A high degree of agreement about the relative severity of each event was reported by Holmes and Rahe who then used the results to derive a scale of measurement for life crisis based on life change units (LCUs). The top of the scale (100 LCUs) is the death of a husband or wife, divorce scores 73, while getting the sack or retiring gets a score of 45. The idea is to obtain an objective count of the incidence of life events in the subject's experience, (usually over a specified period of the recent past) and not to rely on the individual's own selected reconstruction of past problems in order to predict which people are most at risk to serious disorders. It has been used in both prospective (i.e. predictive) and retrospective studies but with only moderate success in identifying the most vulnerable. It appears that threatening experiences are most dangerous to health when they are perceived as such and the attempt to eliminate subjectivity in the SRRS diminishes the predictive power of recent life events as indicators of stress.

Before going on to explore in more detail the sociological literature in this area, it will be useful first of all to clarify the physiological link in the chain of causation leading from life events to disease.

Stress: A Physiological Link in the Social Process of Disease

The simplest biological version of the causal sequence from a state of health to one of illness involves, the invasion of a virus, the response of the body's immune system and the appearance of physical symptoms (see p.14). This aetiological chain could be elaborated to take account of the susceptibility of the potential victim on account of genetic characteristics or acquired immunity. But basically the individual sufferer is, to use Totman's phrase 'A biological black box'.

Everything that affects the sequence is contained in the individual's own physiological condition.

The research that we have just described clearly represents a challenge to this orthodox medical version of how disease happens. It does not fit easily into the usual causal chain because there are no obvious mechanisms for relating social and psychological threats in the production of organic damage and physical disorder. The exception to this is the medical category of *psychosomatic* disease.

The idea of psychosomatic disease depends on the concept of *stress.* This word has become something of an umbrella category covering a wide range of threatening phenomena as well as individual reactions to them. But in its early usage by Selye, it meant an adaptive response in the human body to a stressor, i.e. a threatening stimulus. The response takes the form of a spontaneous secretion of adrenalin, the hormone produced by the pituitary gland. It is easy to appreciate Selye's argument because we are all probably aware from personal experience that threatening situations are likely to produce involuntary physical reactions. In fact the word adrenalin has entered everyday language as a term to depict the felt sensation when stressful situations make greater demands on our bodies. Stress is not necessarily pathological. Stressful stimuli can be quite positive calling up more resources to improve individual performance in a whole range of activities. But if the exposure to a stressor is too prolonged or too strenuous, then the stress adaptation may be dangerous. It was to describe this negative scenario that Selye introduced his concept of the General Adaptation Syndrome: GAS. This is a three step process. Beginning with the excessive secretion of hormones, a build up of corticosteroids in the blood stream occurs to a level which eventually disturbs the correct functioning of the body's immune system and directly damages body tissue. The organic damage which Selye envisaged as the outcome of the GAS, was the bleeding stomach ulcer and this image has filtered down into contemporary popular belief. We have come to see ulcers as *the* typical organic manifestation of stress. But there is growing evidence that stress leads to other kinds of organic damage. It seems that the immune system plays a vital function in restraining the development of tumours in the body, a function that is impaired by the presence of an excess of corticosteroids.

The GAS as Selye described it, has been reproduced in experimental conditions with both animal and human subjects. Following the introduction of a number of different threatening physical stimuli: heat, cold, hunger and electric shocks, a wide range of individual response has been recorded. A major finding of these experiments is that perception and emotional arousal are a key feature of the stress reaction. When the same physical stressor is disguised to make it appear more or less threatening, the response varies according to the degree of mental anxiety that is aroused. Furthermore, researchers have also shown that the GAS is initiated not only in response to physical stressors but to psychological stimuli on their own. So it appears that thought processes are a necessary mechanism of stress, acting as the intermediary between the external stimulus and the body's system of defence.

The discovery of the importance of subjective perception in highlighting stressful experiences opens the door to a much larger range of potential stressors. Among these, we can include the personal crises that sociologists have called life events. From this broader conceptualisation, it is possible to begin to understand why certain biographical experiences seem to be associated with illness and disease. Social mobility, changes of marital status, unemployment and even promotion, have all been identified as risk factors for life threatening disease and it is possible that the causal mechanism is stress. Here we find the missing link between life events and the onset of physical symptoms. The process begins through individual exposure to a stressor which may take a variety of basic forms: physical, psychological or social. To be threatening it must be perceived and defined as such by the subject whose emotions are then aroused, triggering off the stress reaction. This alters the balance of hormones in the body and interferes with the capacity of the immune system to protect the individual. In this state of heightened susceptibility the individual exposed to a disease agent is more likely to succumb. The chain of causation in this version of the disease process is more complex than the model depicted at the beginning of this chapter. It begins with the relationship of the individual with an environment full of potential stressors in a variety of different forms. From there it proceeds in the following hypothetical way:-

Figure 5.2 Stress and Illness

1 **Stressor:** e.g. redundancy.

$\downarrow$

2 **Cognition:** Loss of job equals loss of:- income, means to pay bills and mortgage, status of breadwinner, contact with workmates, everyday routine.

$\downarrow$

3 **Stress:** Excessive secretion of adrenalin and release of dangerous
volume of corticosteroids.

4 **Organic State:** Increased susceptibility through damage to
lymphatic system.

5 **Environmental Exposure:** e.g. to disease agent line influenza virus.

6 **Body's response:** Weakened immune system means no resistance.

7 **Symptoms:** Flu.

This stress model of disease finds powerful support in the research of
Hinkle who has shown that unrelated episodes of illness in the same
person are clustered in specific phases of the lifetime. This suggests
that people are more susceptible to disease at particular periods of
their lives which may be the critical points of biographical experience
when disruptive life events make them more susceptible to disease
agents.

This sequence of interactions between social and psychological
experience and the material fabric of the body itself undermines the
idea of mind and body being separate and autonomous entities. It
recalls ideas about the nature of health and human wellbeing which
were prevalent before the Cartesian revolution which, as we saw in
chapter one (p.13), laid the foundations for the development of the
modern bio-mechanical approach with its emphasis on the organic
properties of disease (p.11). The model of the disease process in
figure 5.2 identifies an important potential role for individuals
themselves in the aetiology of disease. It is through the mechanism of
individual perception that threats become real suggesting that disease
may be prevented if people are prepared to manipulate their ideas
about the significance of threatening events and situations. Equally, it
implies that potential stressors may be found in the social and
economic environment such as, in the above example, the risk of
unemployment.

What can people do to protect themselves from stress in the course
of everyday life? This question can be approached in two different
ways. On the one hand there is the question of whether individuals,

given the right frame of mind, can either avoid a potential stressor or lessen its impact by changing the way they *think* about it. On the other is the question of what scope exists for people to take direct action themselves to either escape the threat posed by a stressful event like redundancy or to get over it once it has happened. Each of these different responses, one based in cognitive processes, the other rooted in social action, have been identified as devices for *coping* with stress.

Coping: The Individual Response to Stress

The concept of *coping* was first introduced by Richard Lazarus to describe the psychological efforts individuals make to adapt to stressful experiences. It proved attractive to others working in the field of stress research and has been applied in a number of different ways. As a result the concept of coping cannot be defined unambiguously. In general it refers to the part individuals themselves play in mediating the relationship between stress at source and the risk of impact on their bodies. Among the diversity of applications, two are of particular interest to the sociological reader. They are:- *coping* as a mental and emotional activity, and *coping* as purposeful action. These two alternative uses of the concept will be referred to as *psychological* coping and *social* coping. This distinction also highlights important variations in the degree of self-consciousness in individual attempts to cope with stress. More self-conscious coping strategies are likely to be initiated at an earlier phase in the potential disease process increasing the chance of preventing any physiological manifestation of stress. Less self-conscious coping is more likely to be defensive in character oriented to the suppression of stressful sensations in the body or to minimising organic damage.

The distinction between psychological and social coping is also associated with other differences of meaning. Conceived of as a strictly mental process, coping tends to carry an implication of personal adequacy or even moral correctness. People who cope do not get ill. Those who succumb to stress, falling prey to illness are by definition non-copers. The event of illness therefore reveals a failure to cope with problems in emotional terms, suggesting a lack of personal control. Social coping does not have this tendency of moral valuation because it is applied to all efforts to deal with stress irrespective of how they turn out. For this reason coping may be initiated at any point in the potential disease process and it may succeed or fail. In terms of the chain of causation in figure 5.2, psychological coping would prevent the onset of disease altogether. Social coping on the other hand points to personal efforts to deal with stress at any of the seven stages in addition to any action taken before onset and afterwards in recovery or adaptation to a chronic condition. It describes all the ways people *try* to overcome their difficulties before symptoms develop, during the course of an illness episode and after it, should it lead to a permanent state of disability.

Coping with Stress: Personality

Lazarus also drew attention to the importance of subjective perception in determining the level of stress attached to any life event. In a famous experiment he demonstrated that the physiological impact, (e.g. increased heart rate), of a disturbing set of visual images of circumcision rites varied according to the sound track which accompanied the film. More soothing music produced lower measurements of physiological stress in the audience and vice versa. It was this that led him to emphasise the role of subjectivity in judgements about stressful experience. He described coping as a secondary psychological device, adopted in the face of a stressful event and designed to reduce stress in the human body and thereby prevent the onset of disease. In his interpretation coping is a summary of the psychological properties of individuals who do not develop disease following exposure to threatening events. Prominent among these, is a sense of self confidence and self esteem. Protected by this psychological armour, individuals overcome events which threaten to overwhelm them because they are willing to redefine them as less significant. Antonovsky, who studied concentration camp survivors, uses coping in a similar way. He defines the capacity for coping as a personal sense of social coherence which enables people to insulate themselves from a stressful environment. For Antonovsky coping is a psychological process in which individuals draw on 'resistence resources' to prevent stressful events from overwhelming them. Resistance resources are made up of flexibility of response in awkward situations and access to close relationships and supportive community.

A central element of psychological coping appears to be the capacity to adapt to change. People who are heavily committed to the status quo and who respond to stress in a 'clinging' fashion are most at risk. Those, on the other hand, who can relax their attachment to any valued dimension of their current circumstances, are better equipped to search for and secure alternative sources of personal identification. Inserting this flexible response into figure 5.2 might take the form of an attempt to rationalise the impending redundancy so it no longer appears threatening to the individual: 'It was an awful job anyway' or 'They did me a good turn forcing me to find some other job better suited to my talents'. Here the threat of job loss is diluted by a reassessment of its value to the individual. The sign that individuals have failed to cope, would be an inability to relinquish the high value they placed on the job about to be lost. Instead of acknowledging the reality of threat and setting about the task of 'neutralising' it, the individual tries to deny it. Knowledge of the impending threat is suppressed and feelings about it are bottled up in a vain attempt to pretend it either will not or has not happened. When the inevitable can no longer be resisted, the individual is left demoralised, depressed and defenceless in the face of whatever agents of disease may be lurking about.

Psychological coping appears as a process of dealing with the stresses and strains of everyday life that is more or less determined by fixed attributes of individuals. The ability to cope by acting creatively to redefine personal circumstances so as to minimise threat is made up of personality traits that have been developed in the past rather then constructed in an impromptu fashion out of whatever resources are encountered in the present. These personality traits are acquired in the process of growing up as people learn to respond to particular situations in particular ways. The part they play as coping mechanisms has been widely researched on both sides of the Atlantic and a number of personality based risk factors for disease have been identified. The most famous example is the so-called 'Type A Personality' possessed by people who are prone to coronary disease. Type A behaviour, originally described by Freidman and Rosenman in 1959, has the following typical characteristics:- over-commitment to work, perfectionism, competitiveness, impatience, aggressiveness and intensive striving for achievement. These forms of behaviour have been repeatedly shown in American studies to be more prevalent among people who develop heart and circulatory conditions: hence the label, the *coronary-prone* personality.

The combined characteristics of this personality type bear more than a passing resemblance to the ideal norms of the protestant work ethic whose adherents are the folk heroes of capitalist civilisation. This suggests that the set of behavioural norms held up as *the* role model for the successful businessman, is actually pathological. The idea that competitive entrepreneurs are more prone to disease is quite a well established folk belief. The most typical candidates for stress-induced ulcers and premature heart attacks, are thought to be 'workaholic' businessmen who sacrifice their health by striving after wealth. The evidence reviewed in chapter 4 casts some doubt on the validity of this belief and in fact research in Britain on the risk factors in heart disease lends no support to the 'Type A' hypothesis.

Marmott's study of heart disease in the British Civil Service, clearly shows that those at greatest risk are the lowest grades of manual workers whose occupational lives offer little scope for the development of 'Type A' traits and who achieve negative ratings on the personality inventory designed to measure them. Marmott concludes that the 'Type A' syndrome probably only applies to middle class white American males.

Even so there have been a great many studies in the United States which identify certain personality traits as risk factors in disease. Some show parallels with 'Type A' behaviours, others seem rather different. Those which conflict despite having also been identified among heart disease patients include, rigidity, overconformism and the tendency to be self-sacrificing. These traits are also found among sufferers from lung cancer, rheumatoid arthritis and digestive disorders and among women with breast cancer strong tendencies to emotional inhibition have been uncovered. While much research remains to be done in this area, it does seem that certain modes of response to stressful events may themselves help to increase rather than diminish the risk of disease.

These various attempts to identify personality traits as risk factors for degenerative disease imply that coping and non-coping are habitual responses invoked day in day out to deal with life in general not just with occasional crises. The scope for personal creativity depends on more or less fixed personal characteristics. A flexible and resourceful attitude to both minor and major life events helps people survive them without 'ill-effect', but survival is largely a matter of personality, not the character of the crisis. This raises the interesting question of how fixed these coping responses may be and what scope exists for training individuals to change the way they handle problems through, e.g. psycho-therapeutic methods.

Coping with Stress: Social Action

The best known British study of coping with disease presents a somewhat less deterministic view of the process. In trying to link life events to the onset of depressive illness in women, Brown and Harris concluded that certain factors mediate between potential stressors (life events), and the risk of disease, acting either to increase or decrease individual vulnerability. Four sources of vulnerability are singled out in the onset of depressive illness. These are:- death of a mother before the age of 14, the absence of close and confiding relationships, the lack of a paid job and the presence of dependent children in the home. Three of these are linked to the stage of the life cycle, while one of them, the loss of the mother in childhood, is a more fixed characteristic of individual women. These vulnerability factors predispose a women to depressive illness only when triggered by disruptive or distressing life events. The process of causation is depicted in figure 5.3.

Figure 5.3 The Link between Life Events and Clinical Depression

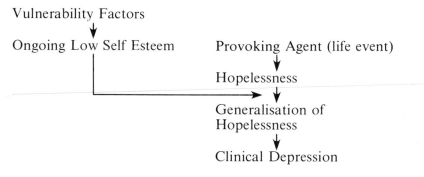

Vulnerability Factors

Ongoing Low Self Esteem   Provoking Agent (life event)

                                 Hopelessness

                                 Generalisation of
                                 Hopelessness

                                 Clinical Depression

Source: Brown and Harris, 1978, p.238.

For Brown and Harris the factors which weaken the capacity for successful coping are not so much descriptions of individual psyche as descriptions of difficult social circumstances or situations. The four vulnerability factors listed above lead to low self esteem which in turn creates a sense of hopelessness. When a person in this situation is confronted with a difficult life event, the reaction is demoralisation and the inability to cope. Low self esteem is not presented as an invariable feature of the woman's personality. It is the product of her current social situation or, in other words, it is a situational phenomenon and not a personality trait. It is encountered in both working class and middle class women but more frequently in the former. The depressed woman in the Brown and Harris study might, in other circumstances e.g. with a job and a supportive partner, experience a greater sense of self assurance enabling her to handle life crises which could lead to depression.

This study stands at the interface between psychological and sociological coping. Its authors emphasise that the origins of disease are largely found in social and economic circumstances. These circumstances have a double edged effect - they determine both the flow of disruptive life events and personal vulnerability. Working class women experience more depressive illness because of relative social and economic deprivation in general (i.e. more life events) which leaves them more vulnerable (i.e. with fewer material and emotional resources). The focus on self esteem as the key mechanism of coping links this study to the psychological approach, but it also shares much common ground with a social action approach.

Apart from psychological adaptation by what other means can individuals avoid or reduce their exposure to stress? This leads us to the other major application of the concept: to individual efforts to manipulate the environment itself rather than merely trying to manipulate ideas about it. This form of coping is an example of social action. It goes without saying that the initiation of action to cope with the problems of everyday life depends on what people perceive and define as problematic in the first place. What this means is that it is subjective understanding which defines whether the individual is inspired and propelled to act. This is how Weber defined social action as behaviour guided by the meaning that individuals attach to it. The social action perspective must be contrasted with the more purely psychological perspective which restricts the process of stress-adaptation to one of only rethinking events.

Coping as social action unites mental, emotional and behavioural reactions into a single process. Although it may be initiated as a thought process, it will only run to successful completion if it results in effective action to neutralise threat. This implies that mental processes on their own, i.e. redefining a threatening event as non-threatening, are unlikely to constitute a sufficient protection for the individual. Reverting to the example of redundancy in figure 5.2, this would imply that the threat of job loss cannot be made to go away purely through an act of mental will, it will only be removed by individual action to get another job. The willingness to be flexible, to view the redundant job as something that can be replaced becomes converted into a successful coping strategy only if this frame of mind leads to energetic job search activities. All this implies the existence of some sense of personal control over immediate circumstances. The redundant worker has sufficient self-confidence to believe that all is not lost, that other labour market opportunities are available. This fits with the focus on self esteem in the Brown and Harris approach. At the heart of successful coping is an image of self as a valuable worker that another employer will want. But what if there are no vacant positions in the economy? In this situation no amount of vigilant social action in pursuit of self interest may be enough to enable the unemployed to protect themselves from the stress of this life event. Indeed the more the unemployed person strives to replace what has been lost in the context of a deteriorating economy, the more stressful the life event becomes. The alternative option, available to a redundant worker in circumstances of high unemployment, is to come to terms with unemployment as a perpetual state of existence. This involves a redefinition of self as a retired person, but it can offer only a limited refuge from the stress of job loss. Quite apart from the economic losses associated with being jobless, there is the normative pressure of the work ethic which makes the unemployed man below retirement age, feel devalued, obsolete and parasitic, if denied the opportunity to work. The individual in these circumstances is caught in a 'double-bind'; whatever he chooses to do, he cannot win. This is because the solution to the problem lies outside of individual control.

Class and Coping in the Negotiation of Stressful Life Events

The last section introduced a new dimension into the process of coping. It revealed that the backdrop to coping activity, conceptualised as it is in highly individual terms, is the structure of society itself. This structure is made up of an unequal distribution of income, property, educational opportunities and qualifications and occupational rights and privileges which favour some sections of society at the expense of others. This patterned inequality shields the more privileged from the worst effects of stress, it leaves some better equipped to cope with events like redundancy, while leaving others totally exposed. This is the link between the management of stress as an individual preoccupation and the pattern of class inequality in the wider society. Coping in sociological terms can now be seen to be a function of social forces and of social structure. It depends on access to resources which can be employed to soften the impact of disruptive life events and provide a breathing space to give individuals time and opportunity to rethink and if necessary reorganise their lives. People best placed to handle transitions of this kind are in any case least likely to experience them. The risk of unemployment is not randomly distributed in the population, it is concentrated among semi- and unskilled workers, the very same groups who are least well equipped in terms of material resources and qualifications, to cope effectively with it. This was the conclusion of Dohrendwend and Dohrendwend in their study of class and race as sources of stress. They argue that the most important determinant of the capacity to cope with life crises is the context in which coping takes place and this is shaped by factors external to the individual which come from the structure of social and economic inequality.

Coping as social action offers important insights into the pattern of health inequality surveyed in chapter 4. It suggests that stress arousal and capacities, strategies and resources for dealing with it must be seen in the context of poverty and material deprivation. Stated in these terms, the concept of the life event seems to lose some of its explanatory power. It does not capture the *pervasive* prospect for stress arousal in contexts of relative social and economic deprivation. A more apt term for the enduring potential for stress in the everyday experience of working class life is *long term difficulties*. Gerhardt following Brown and Harris, argues that it is necessary to distinguish between *loss events* which are essentially personal and involve emotional adaptation, and *long term difficulties* which can only be resolved by purposeful human action.

> In general, psychological and social coping seem to relate to two types of aetiological event: *loss events* which deprive the individual of a loved object or role seem to call for the reconstitution of the person's perception that the world is meaningful, i.e. 'grief work' is required as an adequate form of dealing with the loss. The second provoking agent- *long term difficulties* - seems to call for a different type of coping. Manipulation of and appeal for help to outside sources such as friends, welfare agencies, employing organisations, etc., are required, i.e. attempts at changing one's social rather than one's psychological world. (Gerhardt 1979, 208).

This means that life events are not all of the same character and that differences between them may require different types of coping. From what we know about the distribution of social and economic welfare, long term difficulties can be expected to predominate as sources of stress for working class people while loss events will loom larger (proportionately) for the middle-classes. Even so, loss events would still feature prominently in working class experience.

The concept of long term difficulties appears more persuasive as a means of depicting the onset and development of degenerative illnesses like heart disease and cancer. To explain the pattern of class inequality in age-specific mortality from these causes, involves putting the question not in the terms of: 'Why did X get this disease?' but, 'Why did X get it so early in the lifetime?' In other words why is a member of social class V likely to die of a heart attack a decade before an age peer in social class I; or, why does this body wear out more rapidly than that one? If stress is the physiological link between organic disease and class inequality, then it is much more likely to be an ever present feature of working class experience, whittling away at the fabric of the human body rather than a one-off bout of anxiety triggered by a disruptive life event. This conclusion was reached by DHSS researchers studying the link between unemployment and mortality. Official government statistics provide clear evidence that unemployed men and their wives suffer an increased risk of mortality (see Fox *et al*, 1984). These findings match the observations of Brenner that trends in mortality and unemployment since the beginning of this century are related, that the rate of each rises and falls together. In studying these statistical correlations Stern and others were led to the conclusion that mortality and unemployment are linked through poverty. The people most at risk of losing their jobs in an economic recession are the poorest members of the community who have the highest death rates at every age. The same group experiences the longest duration of unemployment and this means more or less persistent economic insecurity. At times of economic recession this group is disproportionately represented in the ranks of the unemployed which in turn swells its mortality rate as a whole. However it is economic insecurity as a continuous fact of life rather than unemployment as a temporary disruption that it is the primary cause.

Nevertheless it is important to be aware of the fact that loss events are likely to constitute periodical crises for individuals in all social classes requiring varying degrees of emotional adjustment. A typical example of a loss event is death of a close relative or friend. Given the much higher probability of premature mortality in social classes VI and V (p.52), bereavement events are clearly not free of the influence of social class in their incidence. The research of sociologists like Brown and Harris makes it clear that personal vulnerability to, and the distribution of resources for coping with, loss events are highly class related. Figure 5.4 identifies these links.

Figure 5.4 Social Class, Life Events and Coping

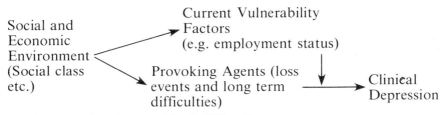

Source: Adapted from Brown and Harris, 1978, p.48.

Coping as social action carried out in the context of a society stratified by class inequalities is likely to mean different things according to where people are located in the social hierarchy. Those with most resources will face fewer life events and have more scope to handle them effectively. Where stressful experience is a much more pervasive feature of everyday life and where opportunities to overhaul everyday circumstances are more restricted, long term adjustment is likely to be rather more defensive in character. Coping may be reduced to rearguard actions designed to ameliorate the effects of stress or even just suppress its physical sensation through resort to medical drugs like tranquillisers or non-medical ones like tobacco and alcohol.

Coping with Stress: Concluding Remarks

The word coping implies that people themselves either consciously or unconsciously, influence their own state of health and even contribute to the onset, progress and outcome of diseases which afflict them. The two major versions of this concept however differ in the extent to which individual motivation is seen as being capable on its own of changing the course of an individual health career. Psychological coping is a mental activity, while social coping unites thought and action into a single activity. In each case there is an implication that ordinary people are not the passive victims of a disease process but may help to bring illness upon themselves by inappropriate responses to stressful circumstances. This chapter has argued that coping should not be analysed in a socio-economic vacuum. The capacity to cope at any level is very largely a product of access to the kind of resources which enable people to exert some degree of control over their circumstances. In this broader sense, the process of coping with stress which threatens to damage the body, offers important insights on the pattern of class inequalities in health examined in chapter 4.

Meanwhile the idea that individual motivation is an important element in outbreaks of disease, has also emerged from an entirely different source in sociology. Talcott Parsons, the most famous American theorist, began his sociological career doing empirical research on medical care. In his book *The Social System* he selects health and medicine to illustrate his ideas on mechanisms of social control. His conclusions on how medicine *functions* to uphold the spirit as well as the physical substance of health will be the theme of the next chapter.

Chapter Six

Medicine as an Institution of Social Control

Medicine and the Social Construction of Illness

What is illness? In chapter 5 a sociological account of the process of illness was presented focusing on personality, behaviour, life events, and class position. This account of how illness happens is of course, only one version of reality drawn from a sociological view of human experience. A medical account of the same process would pick out and emphasise different dimensions. We can predict in a general way what these would be from the bio-mechanical model of illness discussed in chapter 1. It would highlight its organic features, the physical symptoms which prompt the individual to seek out a doctor. The social factors which have priority in a sociological account would fade into the background as attention and effort are directed to the manipulation of visible organic damage.

These alternative accounts, arising from the different disciplinary bases of sociology and medicine, are two versions of the same reality. Neither can claim to capture the whole process of disease or the subjective experience of it. But of the two, medicine is likely to make a much greater impression on what appears real at first hand to the sufferer. This is because people go to doctors to get their symptoms treated and they do not go to sociologists. From the experience of going to the doctor, people learn that sickness is principally a matter of organic disorder because this is what captures the doctor's attention. In this way the *reality* of the illness is interwoven and informed by the experience of being a patient. We have seen in chapter 1 that the effectiveness of medical treatment is generally over-rated. Yet, when things go wrong with our bodies, it is to doctors that we automatically, even 'naturally' turn to for help. We do so because the medical profession occupies a strategic position in society. It is *the* recognised authority on illness and it possesses a virtual monopoly over the practice of healing. This exclusive right, enshrined in Britain, in the Medical Act of 1858, means that only licensed members of the profession may be employed by the state. In the twentieth century, with the growth of the NHS, this monopoly has delivered to doctors almost complete control over all aspects of health care.

In the NHS, the profession has established a network of clinics and hospitals within reach of the whole population and these stand out like the churches and cathedrals of that other once powerful profession, the ministry. Indeed medicine's rise to preeminence has in many ways been accompanied by the social descent of the clergy. Occupying this strategic position in modern society, and surrounded by the symbols of its occupational craft, the medical profession has achieved an unchallenged right to literally define what health and illness are like. In other words our knowledge about health and disease is obtained from medicine, not because it is the scientifically correct version, but because it has secured a position of social influence which has made its own version of what is good for our health *the* orthodox version. This is what is meant by the statement that the social reality of illness is constructed by medicine. Medicine is a social ideology underwritten by the 'neutrality' of science which quite literally defines our understanding i.e. our social ideas, about what health and illness are like. The occupation of doctor therefore is not just a job or a means of income, it is an important social status with power over people and their behaviour. It is in this sense that we may speak of medicine as an institution of social control.

The Sick Role

Going to the doctor is a learning experience. It is the means of transmitting the bio-mechanical model of disease to everyday life. Through the routine contact of doctors and patients in hospitals and surgeries, medical ideology penetrates the subjective experience of illness and herein lies the scope for social control.

> . . . by virtue of being an authority on what illness really is, medicine creates the social possibilities for acting sick . . . its monopoly includes the right to create illness as an official social role. (Freidson 1970, 205-6).

This official social role for the sick person which arises out of the very existence of the medical profession was recognised by Talcott Parsons in *The Social System*. As a systems theorist, Parsons' primary interest was to explain the stability of society as a system of interlocking social roles. The equilibrium of the social system depends on everybody doing a fair share of role playing to keep the system ticking over. Consequently people must be *strongly motivated* by a sense of duty and obligation to their social relationships. Parsons identified sickness as a threat to this sense of interpersonal responsibility because it provides a legitimate reason for people to withdraw from role obligations. For this reason it requires systematic regulation to prevent it being used as an excuse for getting out of customary duties.

This regulation is achieved through the appointment of doctors as (unselfconscious) agents of social control in a process which simultaneously creates an officially sanctioned *Sick Role*. By embracing the sick role, i.e. going to the doctor, the individual sufferer is able to gain social recognition for any symptoms and at the same time society is able to isolate and regulate what might become an outbreak of 'role obligation evasion' which could 'infect' other people. The sick role therefore is an example of *motivated deviance,* a social invitation to temporarily withdraw from role obligations and submit oneself to the officially recognised treatment. In this way Parsons identified in the doctor's role, the important function of maintaining social responsibility among the ill. The silent directive is 'get better quickly because the stability of society depends upon you'. If outbreaks of sickness were left to the whims of individuals in the private sphere of domestic life, they might gradually corrode people's sense of duty to work, to family life, to the community. Only by bringing sickness into the public sphere and encasing it in a system of social control would the risks of role evasion be kept to a minimum.

Vulnerability and Deviance: Two Dimensions of the Sick Role

The sick role is testimony to Parsons' insight on the penetration of social processes into all spheres of human experience. Most people see sickness and disease as biological events somehow apart from societal influence. Parsons' originality in suggesting that they are in essence social phenomena is akin to that of Durkheim when he insisted that suicide was not a matter of individual psychology, but a social fact (see p.79). Nevertheless the sick role has been a controversial concept in the sociology of medicine. This is because of its functionalist character. Parsons implies that the power of professions like medicine to shape ideas and knowledge and to dictate behaviour, are necessary, even good for the maintenance of social stability. He appears to accept the professions' own altruistic propaganda that they are first and foremost oriented to the service of the community not to self interest and that they can be entrusted with monopoly privilege on this account. In his view the necessity for the social control of sickness derives from the needs of the social system and the medical profession is the most appropriate and trustworthy candidate for the guardianship of this function. By other accounts, and Freidson is the leading exponent, the drive to control and dominate the sphere of health and sickness, is found in professional ambition itself and the selfless ideology of community service is little more than a means to this end (see p.112).

The incumbent of the sick role is a patient and, as the word suggests, the expectations of the role are passivity, trust and a willingness to wait for medical help. In other words the sufferer is not held responsible for illness and it is up to others to care for and cure the condition. These expectations arise from the obvious incapacity of the sufferer but also from bio-medical imagery which depicts disease as something that happens to people and not something that is within their control. Getting better therefore cannot be achieved by individuals of their own accord. It involves medical guidance and the requirement that individuals submit their bodies to medical inspection and intervention. This latter necessity is one reason medical work needs social regulation. Quite apart from the awkward necessity to expose one's nakedness to a stranger — a transgression of normal rules of social interaction — treatment itself could lead to irreversible damage, or even death. Combined with the personal insecurity, which the sick already feel on account of worrying symptoms, this makes patienthood a particularly vunlerable social status. In such circumstances, how can people be expected to reach rational decisions about who to consult and what to pay? How, moreover, can society protect the sick from the risk of exploitation by unscrupulous practitioners who might take advantage of their vulnerable position? This is one theme of the social construction of illness. It stresses the innocence of the sick, their passivity in the onset of disease and in treatment, and their vulnerability in the marketplace as consumers of medical therapy.

In contrast to this image of sickness as a status which may be exploited, is one in which it appears as a means of exploiting other people. Since sickness allows people to withdraw from normal social obligations, it provides both opportunity and grounds for the evasion of social responsibilities. This theme is epitomised in the image of the 'malingerer' who fakes illness in order to get out of doing things or the 'hypochondriac' for whom sickness is a permanent but imaginary state of invalidism. These stereotypes of the 'misuse' of illness, are a disguised form of deviance. This is the second theme in the social construction of illness. It stresses the difficulty of identifying genuine sickness and the importance of not leaving it to ordinary people. These elements of the patient role emphasising the need for external intervention and surveillance, give rise to the other theme in the social construction of illness.

Vulnerability and *deviance* are twin dimensions of the sick role and they call for social regulation in two simultaneous directions. On the one hand it is the patient who requires some degree of social protection on account of weakness and vulnerability. On the other, what needs to be guarded against is the risk that the sickness might become a device for evading role obligations thereby weakening the 'motivational' structure of the social system.

Parsons identifies four normative expectations which attach to the *sick role:* two rights and two duties. They are as follows:-

Rights

(1)   Depending on the severity of the illness, an entitlement to some exemption from normal social activities including in extreme cases a requirement to curtail them completely.

(2)   Freedom from personal responsibility for the illness and for recovery. The misfortune of sickness is not the patient's own fault and recovery is not expected to occur through an act of personal will. The patient cannot help it and needs to be taken care of.

Obligations

(1)   Being sick must be viewed as undesirable. This means that the patient must strive to get better. There should be no resignation to the illness state, nor should any advantage be taken of any secondary gains which arise out of being the centre of attention and concern.

(2)   An obligation to seek technically competent help and to co-operate in the process of treatment.

The rights and the obligations are conditional upon one another. The sick cannot expect to be granted time off with sympathy and support if they do not communicate a desire to get well by seeking out the appropriate treatment.

Note how the image of passivity and innocence attaching to the sick person is emphasised as a device to control deviance. By removing individual initiative from decisions about the reality and severity of symptoms, the risk of their being used for subversive purposes can be minimised.

This interpretation of medicine as an agent of social control *functioning* to maintain the stability of society has emerged in some more recent Marxist accounts (see p.122). Naturally they take a more negative view of social stability, i.e. the capacity of industrial capitalism to perpetuate itself without the revolution Marx predicted. To explain the absence of revolutionary fervour in the working class, modern Marxists have unwittingly followed Parsons in a search for the mechanisms of social control which *they* see as necessary to reduce the ideological contradictions of the capitalist system. Medicine is depicted as a means of disguising the unacceptable face of patriarchal capitalism (see p.121). By organising health care around 'atomised' individuals and by focusing attention on the organic dimensions of disease, its real social nature is disguised. Medicine is presented as producing the illusion that capitalism has a progressive technological solution to all ills and it even serves to quell symptoms of rebellion at the kitchen sink through modern wonder drugs like Valium. In consequence ill-health does not become a political issue in the society at large nor is it recognised as the product of conflicting interests in the privacy of family life.

Similar themes are at the heart of Illich's critique of medicine's role in contemporary society. He also focuses on medicine's capacity to deprive people of responsibility for their own health and to stultify personal initiative and willpower for self care. For Illich though it is over-industrialisation and not merely its capitalist variety that is the root cause (see p.47).

Patienthood in Practice

Common to functionalist accounts of medicine's role in society is an image of the sick person as a highly conditioned, passive social actor who has learned to respond obediently to the medical script of illness. The patient looks like the epitome of what Garfinkel called the *Cultural Dope,* an object of manipulation who lacks the will to resist or the imagination to innovate in social relationships. How does this image measure up to the way people actually behave when they get sick? The sick role has proved to be a fertile stimulus to research in the sociology of medicine whose findings suggest that contact between doctors and patients is not quite as Parsons envisaged.

The sick role presents the therapeutic relationship in an aura of harmony and co-operation where the ideal patient is compliant, submissive and co-operative. Consulting room tales tell a different story of conflict, anxiety and tension. Perhaps this is unsurprising given the gap in expectations on each side. As Freidson points out, the typical consultation brings together committed involvement and casual detachment. To the patient the reason for consultation may be pressing, intimate and personally crucial, to the doctor it represents no more than a brief exchange, a drop in an ocean of symptoms to be dealt with as a part of routine work. Given this divergence, disappointment seems inevitable with the doctor appearing impatient and unsympathetic while the patient looks agitated and demanding. Conflict between doctor and patient is widespread. Anne Cartwright in one of her many studies of medical care, reveals that it is doctors rather than patients, who are the most likely to voice dissatisfaction. She found that more than 25% of general practitioners in a survey, complained that over half of their patients consulted for trivial reasons and 56% complained about their lack of humility. It seems that patients do not respect medical judgement as much as they should and they demand treatment as of right instead of requesting it in a deferential manner. This reveals an interesting conceptual contradiction in the sick role. The patient is supposed to defer to the technical expertise of the doctor, to be passive in the process of diagnosis and treatment. Yet, it is patients themselves who have to make the initial decision that their symptoms are serious enough to warrant the call on expert help. The ideal patient from the perspective of Cartwright's dissatisfied GPs, would seem to be resourceful and well informed about symptomatology outside the consulting room, but willing to abandon his fate to medical authority once inside it.

Another conceptual problem of the sick role is the difficulty of identifying the transition between health and illness. It assumes that the transition, while not unproblematic, nevertheless has relatively clear boundaries. Much empirical research on the other hand suggests otherwise. Becoming ill can be an unpredictable, attenuated process in which the difference between being well and unwell is unclear. This means that the sick role is an uncertain status, to be negotiated rather than simply adopted. This is a familiar criticism of the tendency of *structural functionalist role theory* to ignore the problems of entry and exit to new social roles. In this case the issue of role transition is complicated by the fact that it is not at all easy to agree on what constitutes illness. While some sociologists researching the sick role seem to accept the bio-mechanical model with its assumption of the existence of a class of organic illness with identifiable symptoms, others do not. They insist that illness is itself a matter of societal definition much influenced by value judgements about what is normal or abnormal. From their perspective doctors arbitrating the individual entry to the sick role are liable to find themselves exercising moral rather than medical judgement.

The argument that the sick role oversimplifies the nature of the transition between health and sickness is highlighted in research on chronic illness. This is illness which is acknowledged to be long-standing, requiring adjustment to disability and infirmity rather than leading simply to recovery. As a type, long term or chronic illness is much more widespread than the acute type implicit in the sick role. The idea of illness as an acute crisis rather a chronic and persisting state, incorporated in the sick role suggests that Parsons identifies with the professional rather than the lay viewpoint. The bio-mechanical model favoured by the medical profession portrays disease as temporary phenomena, disorders which ought to go away if properly treated. This episodic view reflects more than anything else the episodic pattern of treatment and the profession's indifference to the need to follow up patients who do not return for further treatment. Most degenerative conditions treated in the acute wards of general hospitals are in every sense chronic from the viewpoint of the sufferer.

Chronic illness poses particular problems for the smooth performance of both parties to the sick role. At one level it implies more serious and longer term interference with customary role performance and therefore presents precisely the kind of potential deviance that Parsons saw as threatening to the social system. But equally it leads to difficulties in the therapeutic relationship with which doctors are ill-equipped to deal. By the fact of its persistence, chronic illness has proved resistant to treatment and, by exposing the limitations of medicine, it undermines the technical superiority of the doctor. As a result the therapeutic relationship is likely to be transformed in two ways. Against the shifting background of medical knowledge, the patient may well become more of an expert on his own specific condition than the doctor for whom it is but one of many to be treated on a given day. Secondly, given the failure to find a cure, the only resource the doctor has to offer the patient in exchange for consultation may be a signature on an invalidity certificate, in other words, long term permission for role deviance. Hardly what Parsons had in mind for the purposes of social control. Alternatively, therapy might take the form of counselling, aimed at maintaining the patient's motivation to conquer disability and 'get on with life'. This would fit with Parsons' idealisation of the social control function of medical work but it would hardly fit with the organic ethos of orthodox medicine which leaves doctors ignorant and suspicious of treatment oriented to a mind over matter focus. So it appears that the sick role seriously misconstrues the real nature and duration of sickness as it is subjectively experienced and what medical treatment would look like if it were to be seriously oriented to social control.

Another difficulty lies in the assumption that sickness, venereal disease apart, is a morally neutral category and not the responsibility of the individual sufferer. This is another legacy of the bio-mechanical model with its image of disease being caused by invading alien micro-organisms. In the history of popular ideas about health and illness, this notion is definitely a minority viewpoint. The much more prevalent view has been that victims themselves are partly to blame for their own misfortune. Before germ theory, disease and disability were quite likely to be seen as a divine judgement or as punishment visited upon a sinner. Knowledge about the true mechanism of infection undermined these beliefs in the late nineteenth century. But today the model of the innocent victim is becoming tarnished once more by the growing belief that the onset of degenerative disease linked to smoking or diet is the sufferer's own fault. To the extent that these beliefs penetrate medical treatment they must negate that basic right of Parsons' sick role, that the individual is held blameless.

The lack of fit between the ideal norms of the sick role and research findings on doctor/patient interaction has prompted the development of a number of classificatory schemes designed to explain the variation that has been found in practice. Szasz and Hollander suggest that the relationship of doctors and patients varies according to where it takes place and to the nature of the medical problem involved. They identify three types of therapeutic relationship:-

(1)   Activity/passivity: where the doctor dominates an asymmetrical relationship. This pattern is the role model for the medical emergency where the patient may even be unconscious.

(2)   Guidance/co-operation: the most prevalent pattern where problematic symptoms predispose a co-operative response to medical advice. This is closest to the ideal expectations of the sick role.

(3)   Mutual participation: marked by equality between doctor and patient and found where patients suffer from chronic conditions which involve a great deal of self care.

These three types form a continuum in which the guidance/co-operation model is the mid-point. Clearly where doctor/patient interaction takes the form of mutual participation, the asymmetry which Parsons saw as paramount to the social control function of medicine will be absent.

An alternative classification, developed by Byrne and Long, arranges doctor/patient communication on a continuum of doctor-to-patient-centred treatment. This classification, depicted in figure 6.1, was based on an analysis of a large number of tape recordings of patients consulting doctors. Four styles of communication were uncovered.

Figure 6.1. Doctor/Patient Communication

Silence, listening, reflecting	Clarifying, interpreting	Analysing, probing	Gathering information

Making use of patient's knowledge and experience

Making use of doctor's knowledge and experience

Patient-centred	Doctor-centred

Source: Adapted from Byrne and Long 1976, p.91.

Most studies, including that of Byrne and Long, find that doctor-centred interaction is by far and away the most prevalent form. In the words of one of their doctor respondents,

> The doctor's primary task is to manage his time. If he allows patients to rabbit on about their conditions, then the doctor will lose control of time and will spend all day in his surgery listening to irrelevant rubbish. Efficient doctoring is characterised by a quick clean job.

Getting a 'quick clean job' done in the Byrne and Long survey meant an average of five minutes for each consultation varying from six to four minutes for middle and working class patients respectively. This time difference helps explain why middle class patients were more likely to get patient-centred treatment while their working class counterparts put up with the doctor-centred variety.

It appears then that time as much as anything else constrains the possibility for mutuality in the therapeutic relationship. But there are other obstacles. Another constraint which stands out from research is that doctors deliberately try to keep patients in the dark to make their own job easier. They do so by employing what Goffman called *information control*. By restricting the flow of information about diagnosis and treatment, doctors can cover up uncertainty on their own part, while inducing anxiety and helplessness in their patients. The use of this method for managing patients has been reported by a number of studies. Millman, in a survey of medical errors and their impact on patient trust, concludes that withholding information is the principal means doctors adopt to protect themselves from the possibility of error. The more ignorant the patient about diagnosis and treatment, the less his or her ability to detect mistakes if and when they occur. The reluctance on the part of doctors to provide a free flow of information about treatment is signified by the profession's unwillingness to evaluate the work of colleagues even to the extent of withholding vital evidence about possible negligence.

In studies of satisfaction and dissatisfaction among patients, non-disclosure of information stands out as the running sore of the sick role relationship. Where it occurs it has the effect of alienating patient from doctor and reducing the likelihood that recommended treatment will be followed. This helps to illuminate the reason why, when the doctor respects the patient's feelings, taking what they have to say seriously and sharing information, compliance with 'doctor's orders' is more forthcoming. In more doctor-centred relationships on the other hand, the submissive and compliant posture of patients while on medical premises, may turn into a refusal to 'take the medicine' when they get home. But of course, depending on where treatment takes place, patients do not always have the same degree of choice about whether or not to obey the doctor. The hospital is one site for treatment where opportunities for patient resistance are much less and no account of social control and medicine would be complete without some consideration of this.

The Hospital and the Mortification of Self

The patient's freedom to negotiate a tolerable relationship with the doctor in pursuit of medical advice and treatment, is linked to the power and resources that each can muster. In the community a person has much more freedom of manoeuvre to decide how much time and energy to devote to the sick role. Inside the hospital, the sick role comes to dominate the identity of the person and all thoughts, behaviour and access to other people becomes oriented to the demands of medical treatment.

In a hospital setting doctors possess much more power to make patients conform to their ideal requirements of unquestioning, passive obedience. The rituals of admission seemed designed to communicate this change in the balance of power in the sick role. Goffman, in his study of the manner in which *total institutions* reprogramme their inmates, describes this initiation process as a *mortification of self.* This means quite literally the death of the self. How is it accomplished?

Changes of social status are often accompanied by ceremonies designed to emphasise the transition taking place. An obvious *public* one, marriage, has a clear *rite de passage* which openly displays the change of circumstances of the newly-weds. Other ceremonies are more private experiences, designed to communicate and enforce a change of circumstances to the person directly involved rather than to outsiders. These social transitions are less easily distinguished because they are embedded in things that people take for granted. The process of being admitted to hospital is one of these. It is characterised by a number of procedures designed, in Goffman's words to 'trim and shape' the new inmate for life on the ward. On admission, the person is delivered by kin into the hands of a uniformed member of staff who directs the initiation. Forms must be filled in to create a dossier of personal details — the case notes — open to inspection by staff but not to the patient. Everyday clothing and personal possessions must be removed and taken away to emphasise that escape is impossible. An identity bracelet is attached to the body as a mark of the impersonality of the new environment in which the person will not be automatically recognised. The institution may insist on certain 'cleansing' procedures such as shaving, enemas and bathing which serve to introduce the newcomer to the fact that everyone in white has the right to manipulate the body and marking loss of personal control over it. The whole experience may be summarised as one in which the old identity is taken off and a new one installed marked by an intermediate point of physical and psychological nakedness.

When the patient's kin depart carrying away any personal belongings for which there is no room on the ward, the new patient experiences a sense of being cut adrift in an alien environment in which everyone is a stranger. There may follow, as Coser suggests, a sense of personal betrayal. The family was complicit in the act of incarceration. They co-operated in the removal of personal effects and the new inmate may realise that admission represents a release from the onerous duties of caring for the sick person at home. This may be communicated to the patient emphasising the isolation of the new status and the absence of allies. The asymmetry between staff and patients is marked by the contrast of the starched uniforms and insignia of office of medical and nursing staff to the patient's state of semi-undress. Being perpetually dressed for bed stresses the irrelevance of time, while the scantiness of patient clothing highlights diminishing control over the body.

Goffman stresses that the key feature of a total institution, is the barrier between self and the outside world. As long as a person is at home, even if bedridden, there is some control over daily routine. In the hospital all vestiges of personal power are removed as the person becomes subject to the unpredictable whims of staff. The patient may be left in suspense waiting hour by hour for a chance to speak to the consultant physician, who knows all the secrets of the case and who will determine his or her fate on the ward. The unpredictability of the great one only serves as a reminder that the patient's time does not matter, he or she is at the disposal of medical staff who turn up at their own convenience and not at the convenience of the patient. Daily personal routines, which give structure and meaning to everyday life in the outside world, lose significance inside a total institution. Being an inmate is a twenty-four hour a day preoccupation and the only basis for social interaction. The patient is dissociated from previous sources of social identification. Attempts to draw on past biography, to restore a sense of personal identity, are shunned by staff who are only interested in physical symptoms and have little time to listen to personal reminiscences or look at photographs. As a result the patient is rendered socially anonymous, no more than a bundle of organic symptoms ready for bio-medical processing.

Admission to hospital therefore, by isolating the individual from a community of social support and by systematically denying the relevance of previous bases of social identification, strips the social identity leaving the individual socially naked. As a result, to the fears and anxiety already aroused on account of threatening symptoms a new and equally threatening transformation of self is added which robs the individual of self esteem. It is a process which fits with, even if it is not specifically designed for, the bio-mechanical model of treatment. This model, oriented to the physiology of anonymous human beings and hospital routines, seems designed to sweep away personal social characteristics which get in the way of diagnosis. What are the implications of this process of mortifying the self for recovery and/or the need to adjust to a more permanent state of disability?

From a non-medical perspective the mortification of self would appear to make an illness worse because it heightens the sense of anxiety. Furthermore, by denying the relevance of the patient's social identity in the world outside, treatment in hospital may actually obscure important clues to diagnosis. Elements of self wiped out by the process of conditioning people for life on the ward, may be the very means of understanding how the illness started in the first place. The process could hardly be considered productive in terms of the intended socialisation functions of the sick role, since the patient, deprived of a sense of personal identity and of role obligations, may need resocialisation on discharge in order to pick up the threads of previous life. This might prove even more problematic if, as is often the case, treatment has not been particularly successful and adaptation to a more permanent state of disability is necessary. In these circumstances, the hospital experience may have the effect of adding to the sense of physical disability, a permanent disability of *self*.

Some Concluding Remarks on the Sick Role

Parsons saw the sick role as a means of stabilising society by upholding the sense of duty and obligation that individuals feel towards one another. This is achieved through the institutionalisation of sickness as an official social role to be monitored and controlled by doctors. It means that medical treatment has the object of making the symptoms disappear, not only in the physical sense but also in a motivational sense. The doctor's social control function is to guide the patient back to full participation in society as soon as possible, thereby reducing the length of 'absenteeism' from customary social roles. If Parsons is right, we would expect the medical model of treatment, i.e. the bio-mechanical approach, to be implicitly, if not explicitly tailored to this social control function. This would require that doctors be willing to recognise the importance of the mental as well as the physical dimensions of illness and to extend their therapeutic approach to counselling their patients and encouraging them to conquer physical disability. There is little to indicate either in the structure of the bio-mechanical model itself or in reports of doctor patient interaction, that this is a feature of medical treatment. On the contrary, the strategy of the physician is to emphasise the organic dimensions of illness. Patients are encouraged to wait for the doctor to make them better rather than take any personal initiative themselves. Any counselling performed in primary care in the NHS is carried out, if at all, by social workers attached to clinics and health centres. In the hospital sector which consumes three quarters of the NHS budget, the effects of treatment seem to be designed to destroy self respect rather than to uphold it. Moreover, in judging the achievement of the medical profession in the role envisaged for it by Parsons, we would have to conclude from statistics of sickness absence that it has failed. Since the NHS was established in 1948, the number of days lost through certified sickness, has increased every year and greatly outnumbers those lost on account of industrial disputes (see p.121). Whatever the achievements of the NHS therefore, improvements in 'health' as witnessed by motivation of the workforce, is not one of them.

At the very least this suggests serious flaws in any sociological explanation of the social role of medicine as a means of either upholding the work ethic or, for that matter, the productivity of workers or the profits of their employers. This leads us to consider just whose interests medicine does serve in contemporary society, the subject of chapter 7.

Chapter Seven

The Power of Medicine in Society

Profession or Class: The Roots of Medical Power

What is the source of the power of medicine in society? Among sociologists the answer varies according to which major theoretical tradition they favour. Those influenced by Marx, see power as ultimately rooted in economic relationships. All power in capitalist society flows from the ruling class who own the productive resources of society. By controlling the economy on which the whole population depends for survival, the capitalist class dictates the shape of social institutions and ideas to suit its own interests. Medicine is one such institution. It exercises power over the cultural definition of health and disease; as orthodox treatment it shapes the personal experience of illness and it takes the form it does because it suits the purposes of capitalism.

Marxist theory is sometimes described as economic reductionism. This means that everything to be explained is ultimately reduced to an economic source. A basic distinction is made between the base and the superstructure. The base is the foundation of society. Everything depends upon it. It consists of economic institutions and relationships: private property, the market and classes. Resting on the base are the other social institutions that sociologists study, law, religion, the family, education and so on. In calling these a superstructure, the intention is to convey their superficial nature in relation to the base. They are, moreover, not merely less important than the economic institutions in determining what a society is like, they are actually shaped by the economic base. The family for example, with its gendered social roles, is presented as a development that has come about in response to the logic of capitalism. Similarly medicine is presented as a tool of the ruling economic class. Each is a part of the superstructure, tailored to the needs of capital accumulation, with little autonomy of its own.

This means that medical care, far from being a humanitarian, philanthropic activity, is actually geared to the business of class exploitation. It performs two different kinds of function for capital. Its ideological function is to disguise the true nature of disease and how it is caused. For some Marxists, e.g. Navarro and McKinley, it also plays a more direct part in the process of capital accumulation. It is itself a form of profit making commodity production and, by maintaining the health of the workforce, it also improves productivity and therefore profits. As servants of the ruling class, the medical profession enjoys high economic rewards in return for exercising delegated power. As long as doctors remain loyal to their paymasters, medicine, as a social institution, is secure. The power and privilege of the medical profession results from its value to the capitalist class in maintaining the status quo. But this does not give the profession control over its work: doctors remain the puppets of those who own the commanding heights of the economy.

Other sociologists, less inclined to accept the existence of only one source of power in society, are more likely to trace the power of medicine to other social institutions. For them, politics and ideology are equally important means of generating and exercising power and cannot be reduced to a veneer of capitalist economic interests. This viewpoint is influenced by the theories of the German sociologist Max Weber who, while accepting the power of economic institutions to help determine social organisation, laid equal stress on politics, religion and other social institutions. Contemporary sociologists who take their cue from Weber, are more likely to see the source of medicine's power lying within its political organisation as a profession rather than in any allegiance to the ruling economic class.

Weber was particularly concerned to distinguish what the exercise of power looks and feels like in practice, particularly from the subordinate perspective. He emphasises the difference between the legitimate and the non-legitimate domination by one person or group over others. When the exercise of power carries social legitimacy, it is invested with authority and those on the receiving end are likely to accept their subordination as quite right and proper. When social legitimacy is absent on the other hand, the powerful cannot count on the willing submission of the people they dominate and may well need to resort to naked coercion to get their way. Clearly non-legitimate domination is a much less stable form of power and unsuited to the long term maintenance of social order. How is the means of legitimate domination generated and sustained? Weber identifies three ways:- (1) tradition, (2) charisma and (3) rational-legal authority. The third predominates in modern industrial society. Rational-legal power is the power of office. Its rise to pre-eminence in contemporary society is connected to the growth of bureaucracy, in which power is exercised according to written rules and regulations. It is to this kind of power base that sociologists like Freidson, have traced the origins of medical authority. By this account the power of medicine lies in its political organisation as a profession.

Professional Power and Medicine

Freidson defines a profession as an occupation with a special form of organisation, a special form of legal power (analogous to that of bureaucratic officials), and, in the case of medicine, a special position of dominance in the set of occupations that provide health care in modern society. Unlike many sociologists before him, who were prone to define the professions in terms of the altruistic claims they made for themselves, Freidson argues that the professional ethic of community service should be seen as a device used by occupational groups to obtain exclusive rights to practice. The power of the medical profession lies in its success in having secured, by political means, a legal monopoly over the practice of healing in contemporary industrial society. This made the doctor *the* official expert on health and illness in modern society, a title enshrined in written law. This is the legal-rational base of medical power. It consists of a monopoly, granted by the state, giving the profession exclusive occupational rights, freedom to control the process of recruitment, training and practice and control over the conduct of individual members who each enjoy the right of clinical autonomy. Clinical autonomy means that no lay person can look over the shoulder of the doctor to judge the quality of work and in practice it means that no doctor will ordinarily judge the quality of a colleague's work or even release information that would allow such an evaluation to be made. It is autonomy over the technical aspects of work that Freidson picks out as the essential element of professional power which gives the doctor, in societies as diverse as the USA and the Soviet Union a similar degree of occupational freedom and control over the content of work. For the same reason he suggests that the medical profession is largely autonomous of the ruling class in any society and would be likely to survive any revolutionary social change. What the state has given therefore, it cannot necessarily take away.

Some observers have doubted Freidson's claim that the profession of medicine enjoys similar privileges in the Soviet Union and the United States. They point to the fact that most doctors in Russia are women. This is claimed to be a sign of its weakness. If it were as privileged in the Soviet Union, as Freidson makes out, more men would pursue it. Furthermore, doctors in the Soviet Union are part of the state salariat, they are like civil servants with much less control over the conditions as opposed to the content of work. This suggests that the power of the profession depends upon the relationship of medicine to the state. In both societies the state grants doctors their monopoly of practice but, in the USA, the provision of medical care is largely left to market forces. On this basis we might predict that when medical care is a citizenship right and the direct responsibility of the state, the profession will be less autonomous and more dependent on the political elite for resources. However the situation in Britain would not offer much support to this conclusion. Although more than 90% of medical care is paid for by government, state control over the profession is in some ways less than in the USA. Organised medicine had an outright victory in their struggle with Aneurin Bevan when the NHS was introduced and governments of both right and left have learned to be wary of making it a political enemy. Certainly there is much less scope in Britain for doctors to be held legally accountable for negligence than there is in the United States.

In other ways the situation in Britain is more like the Soviet Union. Compared to other advanced industrial societies, Britain spends less of her national income (approx. 5.5%) on medical care. The government has more control over the total volume of resources devoted to the NHS, because it is directly funded out of taxation revenue. In societies where medical care is paid for through state subsidised insurance such as France (6.9% GNP) or Sweden (7.3% GNP), costs have risen more and consume a larger share of gross national product (GNP). However within the NHS budget, doctors have retained considerable influence over how much goes to specific specialities. Most resources are spent on acute hospitals, the 'high tech' sector. The 'Cinderella' services are the same in all societies. They include services for the mentally ill, the mentally handicapped, the elderly and the chronically sick.

Freidson does *not* pick out technical expertise or esoteric knowledge as a basic source of medical power. Unlike Parsons, who took the technical expertise of the medical profession for granted as a self evident reason for their occupational privilege in the labour market, Freidson argues that a special body of professional knowledge can be generated just as easily after, as before a monopoly of practice has been obtained. If one thinks about it this is necessarily the case. If outsiders were capable of judging the technical merits of the profession's case there could be no claim to autonomy of technique. Both lay public and the political elite alike must take on trust the profession's claim to *know* best. This is why Weber pointed to *legal rights of office* as the source of professional power rather than scientific or technical expertise. The power of medicine is a part of the tendency to bureaucratisation in modern life. It is part of the drive to subject all areas of human experience to rational order and discipline. This leaves us with the question of how an occupational group like doctors was so politically successful?

The Social Rationale for Professional Privilege

We have already hinted, in chapter 6, at the rationale for subjecting the healing craft to professional control. The sick role it will be remembered has two dimensions, deviance and vulnerability (see p.98). It is mainly on account of the second of these that doctors have based their successful appeals for professional monopoly rights.

The sick are vulnerable to exploitation in a number of ways. To begin with techniques of healing are often physically invasive, breaching social taboos of every kind. The doctor claims the right of privileged access to the private body space of the client in order to conduct examinations and carry out treatment which could lead to irreversible damage or even death. This underlines the necessity for some degree of regulation to ensure minimum standards of competence. Equally, given the potential for intimacy in the therapeutic relationship, there is a need for high ethical standards to prevent practitioners from divulging personal information entrusted to them or from getting emotionally or even sexually involved with their clients.

A further problem lies in the asymmetry of the relationship. Patients are supposed to give consent to treatment but in reality they are so dependent on the doctor for guidance that their decisions can seldom be more than rubber stamps of medical advice. Given this asymmetry, patients could be exposed to experimental or risky techniques without even knowing it. This difficulty is magnified by the fact that most forms of treatment carry no absolute guarantee of success so patients seldom have any come back if things go badly wrong. In consequence a high degree of trust is inherent in the relationship. This means that medical treatment is not well suited to being bought and sold in the marketplace, because its customers cannot be expected to exercise the 'natural instinct' for striking a good bargain that they use when purchasing other forms of personal service. This explains how doctors succeeded in obtaining a public monopoly over the treatment of sickness. The key to their political success was to join together into a single profession which could be clearly identified and which claimed to offer a uniformly high standard of competence and ethical conduct. By sheltering under the reputation of their profession, doctors appear to the public as a standard product, equally skillful and equally trustworthy. Given the absence of any systematic evaluation of medical technique, it is virtually impossible to demonstrate medical incompetence, and the occasional expulsion of deviants who break the medical code of practice serves to uphold the fundamental integrity of the profession as a whole. In Britain, the medical profession has shown itself more willing to punish unprofessional behaviour than its sister profession the law. This pragmatism is a sign of political skill. The law society, by defending indefensible cases of malpractice, has made the legal profession vulnerable to its critics, with the result that some of its privileges e.g. the conveyancing monopoly, have been put at risk.

The interpretation of professional power and privilege as the outcome of political action, must be clearly distinguished from structural functionalist explanations which accept the profession's benign self image as well as the claim that public and professional interest are one and the same thing. For Freidson, the first and foremost goal of the profession is to serve the interests of its members and there is no necessary identity between these and those of the general public. This contrasts with Parsons' vision of the patient as the prototype of the professional client, a classic case of vulnerability and dependency whose needs cannot be catered for in the context of open-market competition. From this viewpoint the inherent risk of granting monopoly rights to an occupational group (that their prices will rise in the absence of competition) is offset by the fact that doctors, like all professions have a vocational orientation that is altruistic. This means that they are basically oriented in their work to serve the community rather than to personal gain. In medicine this means the Hippocratic Oath which enjoins doctors to do all in their power to help the sick irrespective of material interest. This selfless quality of putting the client first, is in addition to the other occupational attributes which Parsons argued were a general feature of the division of labour of industrial societies. These include: achievement values, universalism, functional specificity, and affective neutrality. Borrowing Freidson's translation of these, what this means in terms of medical practice is that:-

> . . . it is expected that physicians be recruited and practise on the basis of ability rather than ascribed characteristics, that they rely on generally accepted scientific standards rather than on particularistic ones, restrict

their work to the limits of their technical competence, work objectively without emotional involvement, and finally, put the patient's interests before their own. (Freidson 1970, 159).

These are the reasons doctors themselves advance in defence of their exclusive rights to practice. Some economists, notably Milton Friedman, have argued that professional claims to protect clients are fraudulent. They make the practice of medicine inefficient and non-accountable, in short, the best closed shop in the labour market. The experience of the NHS suggests that there is some force to this criticism given the many forms of treatment which are not properly evaluated either before being introduced or even after they have been in use for a long time (see p.9). This points to a problem in both Parsons' and Freidson's explanation of the power of medicine. One would expect that in granting a legal monopoly the state would expect the profession to demonstrate some degree of occupational competence and effectiveness in practice. Yet, if medical opinion rather than scientific fact (see p.8) is how the profession operates today, over a century ago when it obtained its legal privileges from the British State, there would have been even less to go on in terms of effective therapy.

Freidson argues that a *consulting* profession must be capable of demonstrating some degree of effectiveness with a lay public in order to sustain professional integrity and public confidence. *Scholarly* professions like university professors are insulated from the public and do not need to justify their privileges in the same way. In the light of present day knowledge, it is difficult to see how the proven effectiveness of medical expertise could have formed any part in the profession's bid for legal privilege.

However treatment is only one aspect of the medical task. An equally important goal of medical consultation, for both doctors and patients, is diagnosis. People in the throes of a health crisis need to know what is wrong even though they may be disappointed when the medical judgement is announced. In this respect, the limitations of treatment itself are less relevant than professional skill at description and classification.

In Britain the period in which the profession was consolidated was one characterised by substantial social and economic change. Industrialisation had led to the growth of a new class of middle-income occupations which provided an enlarged clientele for doctors. It was also a growth period for hospitals which at the time were primarily places for medical training and the care of the destitute sick. The spread of hospitals and institutions like them for incarcerating the sick and needy, led to a growing need on the part of the state for trustworthy employees who could supervise them, which in turn expanded occupational opportunities for doctors. How was the state to distinguish the trained doctor from the quack? The 1858 Medical Act by insisting that only members of the profession need apply for state salaried positions, provided the answer to this question.

The period was also one of great optimism about science and technology. Even if medicine had yet to find a means of converting new scientific knowledge into effective therapy, as the standard bearer of science in the field of health care, it was probably assumed that it was just a matter of time. As the Victorian middle classes began to realise the scope for taking their future into their own hands, they would naturally believe that health was a suitable sphere for professional intervention and should not be left to divine fate. The profession also undoubtedly benefited from being associated with public health innovations which, although they had nothing to do with medical treatment as such, were nevertheless sometimes due to the inspiration of medical practitioners like Snow (see p.15). It was in this historical context that the British medical profession 'earned' its legal monopoly of practice.

Is there a Link between Medical Power and Capitalism?

In the twentieth century, doctors have become the most powerful, the most respected and the best paid professional group. In terms of their economic position, their education and life style, they seem to be part of the richest and most privileged class in society. This has led some writers to conclude that medical power itself derives from the profession's membership of the ruling economic class.

McKinley, in an analysis restricted to the organisation of health care in the USA, argues that medicine is a fully fledged part of commodity production under capitalism. He asserts that the *logic of capitalism* i.e. the drive to accumulate profit, has penetrated and overwhelmed the delivery of health care. The lack of demonstrable effectiveness of treatment, discussed in chapter 1 is a direct outcome of this. Treatments on offer in 'high tech' hospitals are there because they are profitable and any benefit to the sick person is quite coincidental. 'Consequently the House of Medicine under capitalism will never contribute to improvements in health unless such improvements facilitate an acceptable level of profit'. (McKinley 1977, 462).

For McKinley then, there is no difference between the production of the usual capitalist commodities, cars, washing machines, hot dogs, hairdressing and open heart surgery. The underlying logic of the manufacture of all these goods and services is the search for and seizure of profit. The real profit of medical practice is creamed off by:- (1) the large corporations which manufacture medical supplies, (2) the insurance companies which insure people against the potential 'misfortune' of both disease and treatment and (3) the owners of private hospitals who charge exhorbitant rates for in-patient treatment. This is why McKinley defines the majority of doctors as workers who are 'productive for capital'. Although their labour is 'socially wasteful' in that it does not fulfill real needs or contribute to human welfare, it is highly profitable. Doctors are therefore part of the subject class. They are there because they '. . . return even more value in the form of social surplus than they receive in the form wages'.

McKinley's thesis is directed as a critique of Freidson. His object is to show that medicine has no autonomy, that it is under the thumb of capitalist interest. Because medical treatment is so attractive to capital, doctors lose control and autonomy over the content of their work, finding themselves obliged to devote *most* effort to ineffective but profitable treatment. This means that medical science itself comes to neglect the most important health problems of the population. McKinley's model of the forces dictating the character of modern medical treatment depicts medicine as a dependent client of capital, a relationship negotiated by the state which grants the profession its monopoly.

Figure 7.1 Forces Determining the Character of Modern Medicine

1.   Capital

                              |

                          determines

                              ↓

2.   State

                              |

                          governs

                              ↓

3.   Medical Profession

                              |

                          dictates needs of

                              ↓

4.   Public

Capital is the principal factor determining the nature of medical care in modern society. The other three levels are ranked hierarchically in order of decreasing importance. At the bottom, we find the dependent and guileless public who are presented as the willing human sacrifices on the alter of profit-oriented medical care. The medical profession are also a subject class in this model. Their control over their work conditions which features so prominently in Freidson, is illusory. Their work is ultimately just another form of commodity production subject to the logic of capitalism.

McKinley supports his account by pointing to the enormous profits generated from medical treatment in the US. He quotes the figure of $139 billion (8.9% GNP) as the total output of the medico-industrial complex in 1976. With all this money swimming around, McKinley finds the appeal of a Marxist interpretation irresistible. That medicine in the US is highly profitable is indisputable, but does this mean that that profitability is the principal force shaping what treatment is like?

The view of the medical profession as part of the subordinate class whose rewards do not represent the full value of their labour, is certainly novel. But in McKinley's application of Marxism to the medical industry in the US, the site of exploitation is not so much the human labourer as the human consumer. In other words the patient seems more exploited than the doctor. Nothing could be further from Parsons' view of this most vulnerable of social statuses requiring special protection in market society. In McKinley's account, the state acting as the executive of the ruling class, turns this vulnerability into a profitable business angle corrupting the healing profession into the bargain.

Can we accept this argument that the logic of capitalism determines every aspect of social organisation to the extent in this case of completely distorting the entire healing art/science? Certainly the USA provides the best example for the elaboration of the case. Other varieties of capitalism where the distribution of medical care has not been left to market forces, offer much less support. In Britain, virtually all investment in medical treatment comes from public funds and the scope for profiteering is very much less. Even so, the character of medicine is much the same in both societies suggesting that the criterion of profitability is not the major determinant of medical knowledge and technique. Doubting the validity of McKinley's position does not involve the denial of the existence of a profit orientation in the manufacture of medical supplies. But saying that profits can be made out of medicine does not lead to the conclusion that the businessman's greed for profit ultimately determines medical

MERTHYR TYDFIL COLLEGE
LIBRARY

judgement and the treatment of patients. In McKinley's own words, 'the game would have little public appeal and could even be cancelled if the star players were absent' (p.467). This underlines the need to distinguish the real sources of the power of medicine from the mere fact that capitalist enterprise can cash in on it. Where health care is left to free market forces, medical work will undoubtedly favour forms of treatment which offer the highest rewards to the profession. But just because doctors can demand high salaries or fees does not mean that medical power is economic rather than political or ideological in *origin.*

Furthermore, to accept McKinley's case involves agreeing with an extremely pessimistic view of humanity. In his model, the consulting public are presented as a manipulated mass, hardly promising material for the fulfilment of the historic proletarian mission of liberating humankind through the inauguration of democratic socialism. This portrait of individuals painted by McKinley, is 'over-socialised' man, programmed to think and act in ways dictated by society. What it fails to take account of is the tendency of contemporary capitalism to raise individual consciousness and make people believe that they can and ought to exert more control over their circumstances and destines. The growth of individualism is the reason that challenges to the medical domination of ideas about health have begun to take shape in capitalist rather than collectivist or socialist societies.

In a classical Marxist sense, the capitalist class is distinguished by its ownership of the means of production and its economic position is sustained by making profit out of the labour of the working class. Clearly the medical profession does not fit easily into the picture of class relationships in this orthodox sense. They do not own productive property as such nor do they extract surplus value (i.e. profits) from workers in any direct way. However, Navarro argues that medicine aids the process of capital accumulation in an indirect way. By improving and maintaining the health of the workforce, medicine expands the productivity of human labour and thereby increases the volume of surplus value that may be extracted from it. Ironically the working class itself is seen as helping this process along. In making free medical care an object of class struggle, workers themselves have persuaded the state to subsidise wages and increase profits by relieving the employer of the burden of compensating workers directly for the damage to their health incurred by capitalist production.

A shortcoming of this interpretation is the false assumption that medicine has been and is responsible for improving human health. We have seen that there is no evidence to support this assumption. If anything, there is more evidence to support the opposite conclusion that medicine has helped reduce the productivity of the labour force in their official capacity as gatekeepers to the social security system. Since 1948, general practitioners have certified an ever increasing volume of 'time off' for sickness suggesting that the NHS has undermined the health of the workforce rather than improved it.

Table 7.1 Certified Sickness Absence in the UK

Year	Days Sickness Certified Per Man.
1954	12.8
1960	12.8
1962	13.2
1964	13.9
1966	14.5
1970	15.8
1973	16.2 (As % of 1954 = 127%)

Source: Adapted from *On the State of Public Health (1976)* HMSO, 1977. Adapted from table 2.5, p.30.

A more persuasive interpretation of the link between professional and class power sees medicine as acting as an ideological support to the capitalist system. Navarro calls medicine 'an ideological state mechanism' serving to mystify the real exploitative nature of capitalism and allowing the system to perpetuate itself. This interpretation, in common with other modern Marxist attempts to elaborate a *political economy of health,* starts from the premise that capitalism is the source of most if not all of the afflictions of human beings in the advanced industrial societies. From this perspective, what needs explaining is why the working class have not figured out how awful the system is and embarked upon the process of overthrowing it. The answer is provided by the Marxist concept of false consciousness. The working class have been lulled into a false sense of security which prevents them from recognising their true material interests. Medicine appears as an instrument of class rule in this explanation. It creates the illusion of a clever and caring society which is oriented to save human life. In focusing on the organic end product of disease, medicine deflects attention away from its causes in economic life. It thereby prevents health from becoming the political issue and potential force for social change that it would otherwise be.

All theoretical explanations have their limitations and this is no exception. The political economy of health thesis has a tautological character. This means that its conclusions are fashioned to provide a solution to a problem of its own making. The problem is: why is there so little class consciousness about the damage to human health caused by capitalist methods of production and distribution? The answer is: the capitalist class have incorporated the dominant healing profession within their ranks in order to use them as a means of disguising the way in which human health is corroded by a market society organised around the profit motive. But does capitalism have that much to hide? In relative terms, health has improved continuously under capitalism so that an alternative explanation might be that the ruling class has undersold itself. It has been duped by the medical profession along with most people into believing that doctors were responsible for bringing about improvements in health. In fact as we saw in chapters 1 and 2, the reduction of mortality in the nineteenth century was more likely to be linked to the growth of industrial capitalism in Britain than it was to anything connected to medicine as individual therapy.

This version of the political economy of health thesis suffers from a basic inability to show that capitalism as such is the cause of disease in modern society. There is no evidence to show that health in capitalist society is systematically worse than it is in socialist societies or any other kind of society for that matter. If anything, advanced capitalist societies have a better record in the post-war era than their collectivist neighbours in Eastern Europe (see p.38). While rates of mortality have continued to fall in most European societies, those in the West have fallen faster and further than those in the East. An exception to this is the Soviet Union, the only industrial society to actually witness increases in the mortality of citizens of all ages including infants. Since 1976, when the upward trend was clearly evident, the USSR has declined to supply any further statistics to the World Health Organisation (cf. Davis and Feshbein, 1981).

This suggests that the ruling class in capitalist society is not on the defensive to the extent that writers like Navarro presuppose. This in turn means that the need for agents of mystification, a role in which, by all accounts, the medical profession is in a class of its own, is overrated. This is not to argue that there is not an accommodation between the ruling profession and the ruling class. It is quite evident, for example, to take the case of the drug companies, that massive profits can be made out of the medical monopoly. But a handy alliance does not reduce professional power to an offshoot of capital. This leads us back to the possibility that the power of medicine in contemporary society is not just an adjunct of capital but has an autonomy all of its own.

Professional Autonomy and Health Policy

Freidson argues that *occupational autonomy* is the key to understanding the power of the medical profession in contemporary society. All occupational associations including trade unions seek to secure greater autonomy for their members. Few, if any, have been as successful as the medical profession in capturing complete control over the conditions of work, including a virtual guarantee of non-interference from outsiders. This occupational privilege is further strengthened in most industrial societies by the fact that medical care has largely been removed from the cash nexus. In consequence most patients do not pay the doctor directly for services provided. The paymaster is either the government or an insurance company with the result that there is less scope for accountability in the case of unsatisfactory treatment. In Britain the state pays for medical care mostly from taxation revenue. Treatment is free and general practitioners receive an annual capitation fee for each patient, irrespective of the quantity or quality of treatment provided. This tends to convert the delivery of medical care into a sort of free gift passing from the doctor to the patient in a manner which underlines the subvervience of the recipient and the autonomy of the donor. The separation of the client from the process of payment may help to explain why the costs of medical care have rocketed well above the inflation rate, particularly in those societies where the insurance principle prevails.

In most advanced industrial societies, standards of health and health care are in part the responsibility of government, and political parties seeking election include health policy in their manifestos. However the existence of powerful professional interests severely restricts the room for political manouvre. How can politicians judge what is best for the nation's health? They lack the means to evaluate the prevailing claims of medicine and the absence of any independent evidence for assessing the effectiveness of treatment (see p.8) makes them dependent on the members of the profession for advice and guidance. The scope for conflict between politicians and the profession is minimised by the fact that medicine exerts great influence over popular ideas about the nature of health and illness so that professional aspirations tend to be synonymous with those of political parties. Debate takes the form of how much GNP should be spent on health (i.e. medical care) rather than focusing on issues which present any serious challenge to the status quo. This means that political parties seldom question the wisdom of tying up most resources earmarked for health in curative medical treatment. But when struggles over the use of resources do arise, the profession usually emerges victorious. The history of the NHS provides some illustrative examples of the triumph of professional autonomy in practice.

The introduction of the National Health Service in 1948, was the culmination of a bitter struggle between the Minister of Health, Aneurin Bevan, and the medical profession. The idea of a comprehensive system of health care had gained credibility during the war through the formation of the Emergency Medical Service and the publication of the Beveridge Report (1942). Before the end of hostilities, a number of discussion documents and proposals had been put forward by Liberal and Tory health ministers in the coalition government. These early plans included the proposal that doctors become salaried employees of the state. This was rejected by the profession who saw it as a threat to autonomy. The National Health Service Act of 1946, the enabling legislation for the new service, deliberately left vague the question of how doctors would be paid. Bevan favoured the idea of medical state salariat but knew it would be the major sticking point for the profession. According to Michael Foot, his biographer, he always intended to let the profession have their way, but judiciously left the question open so that it could be a point for negotiation and compromise on his part.

In the ensuing struggle Bevan allied himself to the most prestigious spokesmen for the profession, the leaders of the Royal Colleges, who represented the interests of the consultants in hospital. This elite section of the profession was not opposed to the idea of salaries which they had become used to during the war. Their recent experience of greater state intervention in the hospital sector enabled them to see the direct benefits to be gained from a stable source of finance. At this time many of the hospitals in Britain were funded by a mixture of charity and public funds. With the growth of new technology this source of finance was proving to be precarious and insufficient. During the thirties a number of financial crises had only been averted through the intervention of the state and many hospital specialists realised that a general take over was only a matter of time. In consequence they were natural allies for Bevan in his task of persuading the whole profession to come into the NHS. In the final compromise, the hospitals were taken into public ownership and the consultants became either full or part-time employees of the state. They even enjoyed the privilege of being able to use the enhanced resources of the publicly owned hospitals for private fee-paying patients. In addition a system of secret merit awards was introduced to provide some means for the leaders of the profession to reward what they took to be high standards of excellence. The general practitioners remained as fee-paid independent contractors: free to decide where they would practice, to arrange their own hours of work and to provide their own premises.

This agreement left the medical profession with a great deal of control over, not only their immediate conditions of work, but also over the definition of the priorities of the new service. It is unclear how far Bevan was aware of the power he had surrendered to the profession in 1948. At the time he declared, 'My job is to give you all the facilities, resources, apparatus and help I can and then to leave you alone as professional men and women, to use your skill and judgement without hindrance'.

In practice this meant that the National Health Service became a comprehensive medical service or, as some critics have put it, a national disease service, oriented to the treatment of symptoms and not to preventing disease or promoting health in any positive sense. The profession retained substantial control over the management of the service and inequalities in the provision of services between different parts of Britain which were evident before the war remained just as marked thirty years later (see p.60). These inequalities were the product of the haphazard development of voluntary hospitals set up on the proceeds of charitable trusts and bequests. A nationally organised system of medical care ought to have equalised variations over the country, but it did not. The budget for the service instead tended to be allocated according to historical precedent, so that areas best endowed in 1948, continued to be so when the government took over responsibility for finance. Bevan's aim was to provide equality of access to medical care across the country as a whole, but he did not establish a central means of control that was capable of resisting the profession's desire to maintain things the way they were. In effect, by gaining control of the NHS in this way, the profession consolidated its power making it virtually unassailable.

It is interesting that Bevan, the health minister of the 1946 Labour Government, recently elected in a landslide poll, did not question the assumption that health care was synonymous with medical treatment. He seemed to share the belief of Beveridge, that there is a finite quantity of disease in the population. In 1948, it was anticipated that the high initial costs of the NHS would gradually fall as people became healthier under its influence. This forecast proved to be disastrously incorrect and within a few years, a Royal Commission was set up to inquire into the reason for rising costs. Since then the same trend has continued despite government economies. The continued growth of expenditure reflects the expansion of the medical profession, the introduction of new specialisms and forms of treatment often involving expensive technological equipment and, not least important, demographic trends (in particular an ageing population). The impact of advanced medical technology on the health of the population as a whole is not understood with any precision. What can be said is that it is not very great (see chapter 1). Nevertheless, according to the distribution of merit awards for excellence of achievement, high technology medicine appears to be the area the most valued by the leaders of the profession. Merit awards are secret payments made to selected consultants in the NHS on the advice of a professional committee. In 1977, while more than 60% of cardiologists and neuro-surgeons received these awards, effectively doubling their salaries, less than 30% of specialists in geriatrics or mental health were so lucky. The greatest rewards in terms of both salaries and resources for practice, go to the sector where the feats of 'heroic' surgery take place. Perhaps the profession has realised that there is nothing like an occasional mircale for sustaining public confidence in routine medical treatment.

However, there are signs of an increasing awareness of the limitations of medical treatment. These have come from within the profession as well as from outside of it. Critics accept that most serious disease afflicting people after the age of 50 is more amenable to prevention than to cure. Equally the disabling conditions of old age which increase as the population ages, require nursing and counselling rather than medical attention. But redirecting the priorities of the NHS has proved to be a near impossible task. Successive priority documents published by the DHSS (Department of Health and Social Security) have called for a redistribution of the budget to favour community care for the 'cinderella services'. They argue for the contraction of the hospital sector and an expansion of domicilliary care, enabling people to be cared for in their own homes instead of being incarcerated in long-stay hospitals. But they have never been put into effect by the regional and district health authorities directly responsible for NHS expenditure. In the period since 1970, the hospital sector has continued to expand at the expense of the underprivileged community sector as Figure 7.2 reveals. Alaszewski and Haywood, in a study of how these national priorities get subverted in the process of local decision-making, conclude that the blockage is to be found in the principle of *clinical autonomy*. District treasurers and administrators faced with powerful local consultants who insist that their resources be maintained or even increased, have no means of challenging 'clinical judgement'. To do so would be tantamount to claiming that they know better than the doctor.

Figure 7.2 Selected Health Service Labour Power Statistics, 1959-1973

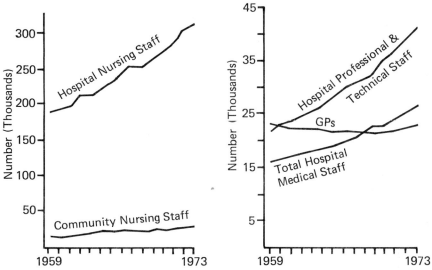

Note: Whole-time equivalents are used throughout except in the case of hospital nursing staff and GPs where actual numbers are given.

Source: *Health, Money and the National Health Service* by P. Draper, G. Best and J. Dennis, p.34 (Unit for the Study of Health Policy, Guy's Hospital Medical School, April 1976).

These national statistics indicate the increasing share of the NHS budget consumed by the hospital sector. The tale they tell is of a decentralised system of decision-making in the NHS, heavily influenced by powerful clinical interests, who get their own way despite central directives from the DHSS.

Concluding Remarks: Whose Interests does Medicine Serve?

In every advanced industrial society, the medical profession enjoys monopoly privileges in the labour market. These privileges have been secured from the political elite of each nation state with the result that medicine is, in large measure, an international profession. Its practitioners are highly paid, highly respected and they enjoy a great deal of control over the conditions of their work, even to the point of being insulated from criticism and accountability. The power of the profession in society at large is not merely the sum of the occupational privileges of each doctor. Individual privilege flows from the position medicine occupies as a social institution in contemporary society. As a social institution, medicine is rather like a secular religion. It is the received wisdom on matters of life and death as well as on physical and spiritual welfare. Its esoteric knowledge has the characteristic form known as the 'bio-mechanical model' and because of the power of the profession, it is *the* orthodox way of thinking about health and organising the delivery of health care. Naturally this means that in Britain, the medical profession has captured the National Health Service. Control over the NHS gives doctors 5.5% of GNP to spend on their professional activities. This has meant that the development of health care over the post-war era has been dominated by cure-oriented, hospital centred treatment, with a corresponding neglect of prevention and a devaluation of the caring dimensions of healing relationships.

The power of the profession has an explicit legal form. It is enshrined in the statutes of each separate nation state and this implies a certain level of dependence on political elites. In other words, medicine got its exclusive mandate from the state, and what the state has given, the state could conceivably take away. However, the prospect of the ruling elite in any society attempting to withdraw the exclusive license it issued in the past, is not very great. In Britain, the profession has enjoyed its monopoly for over a century and during this time it has gradually imposed its own version of the meaning of health and health care on the population. This book has argued that there are a number of regressive features in modern medicine: the singular focus on cure rather than care or prevention; the mind/body dualism; the tendency to ignore the influence of behaviour and environment in preference for taking the abstract individual as the site of disease; the obsession with the manipulation of organic symptoms through chemical and mechanical means; and the treatment of patients in the isolated, even mortifying, environment of the hospital. Remember these negative dimensions of contemporary medicine are not the unfortunate but unavoidable side effects of successful treatment. They are the core of the profession's occupational skill and the NHS is organised to deliver health care according to this professional recipe whose contribution to present standards of health has never been carefully evaluated but is known to be very limited.

Nevertheless the profession's version of what health and disease are like, is written into our culture. The bio-mechanical approach is literally interwoven with everyday beliefs about why sickness occurs and what must be done about it. This means that the profession has greatly consolidated its power base in society. Skilfull political organisation was its original route to power, but in becoming an orthodox body of cultural belief, a new ideological dimension has been added which makes the profession virtually immune to outside interference. It is possible that doctors are more powerful in Britain than in other industrial societies which have continued to allow the market to intervene in the provision of treatment. By gaining control of the NHS, doctors find themselves offering free services to people in need. The gift-like dimensions of the professional art in this country must also serve to build public support for the profession and to further weaken the scope for any government to take back any part of the medical monopoly. Medicine's power in contemporary society is therefore built out of a combination of political organisation, ideological domination, and control over the infrastructure of public resources for health. To reform health care would involve action to weaken the medical power base on each of these fronts and the most important preliminary would be to dilute the power of medical ideas in our culture by exposing their limitations. Herein lies the real message for health education.

This explains how doctors sustain their powerful position in society, but in whose interests do they exercise their power? This chapter has provided three possible answers to this question. Parsons sees the medical profession acting to protect the public interest by upholding high standards of treatment. We have seen in earlier chapters that health care fashioned according to the bio-mechanical model has serious limitations and, in this chapter, that attempts to reform it in the direction of prevention and domicilliary care, are invariably blocked by professional autonomy. It is clear from this that the promotion of better health in the population is not the profession's overriding concern. If it was, the NHS would devote far more resources to disease prevention than it currently does (less than 1% in 1982). This suggests that altruism towards fellow human beings is not a particularly important force behind the development of professional medicine. This in turn means that it is inappropriate to locate the objectives of the profession's bid for power in something called community service.

More significant for Parsons, is medicine's role as an agency of social control. Good health is a functional pre-requisite for society and 'health' for Parsons, means the satisfactory performance of social roles. Medical treatment is presented as a mechanism for maintaining the individual's sense of commitment to social roles and of responsibility to other people. It therefore helps to maintain the high levels of social co-operation which are necessary in advanced industrial society. To Parsons therefore, medicine exercises its power in the interests of society as a whole.

We saw in chapter 6 that empirical studies of doctor/patient relationships offer little support to Parsons' typification of the sick role. Moreover, the statistics of sickness absence suggest that access to free medical care has, if anything, led to an increase in absenteeism rather than acted, as Parsons would predict, to uphold the work ethic. There is an important sense in which organised medicine serves as a preservative of social solidarity, but it is not the one which Parsons had in mind. Since the war, the NHS has been the primary symbol of citizenship in Britain. By promising to treat everyone in an equal fashion, it stands as a testimony to the idea of social equality in a democratic society. This was an explicit intention on the part of its founders and like other features of the welfare state, it has helped to bind the political consensus that our own form of society is the best currently an offer.

Navarro's view of the objects of medical power shares certain similarities with Parsons, although in other ways, it is radically different. Like Parsons, he sees medicine performing a conservative social *function*. It is principally designed to preserve the social system. The explanation of social institutions in functionalist terms is the hallmark of Parsonian social theory. In Navarro, we see a Marxist inspired version, an example of what Mishra calls 'left functionalism'. Navarro finds medicine serving to maintain the stability of the capitalist system, by maintaining the health and productivity of the workforce while dampening down social protest. This last function sees medicine as an 'ideological state mechanism', with the profession acting as the public relations arm of the ruling class, obscuring the real causes of disease in order to make the system appear more attractive than it really is. This view echoes the memorable pronouncement of Balfour at the turn of the century that social legislation is not merely different to socialist legislation, it is its most direct and effective antidote.

Navarro's interpretation of the purposes medicine serves makes use of the fit which exists between high technology medicine and the dominant character of industrial capitalist civilisation. He draws out the essential features of the bio-mechanical model and uses them to show how the profession disguises the real environmental and occupational nature of disease under capitalism in a false model of individual pathology. The bio-mechanical model is not an isolated feature of contemporary culture. As chapter 1 argues, it reflects the individualistic and technological ethos of advanced industrial civilisation. For this reason it could be argued that there is a natural fit between contemporary medicine and industrial capitalism. While this may be correct, it does not explain why professional medicine fits perfectly well, and for that matter helps to sustain, other kinds of social organisation which are far more collectivist than capitalist in character.

Both Navarro and Parsons provide 'functionalist' accounts in which medicine appears primarily as an institution of social control maintaining the stability of society. Where Navarro and Parsons part company is over the purpose of theory. For Navarro the purpose is not just to explain social order and stability but to disturb it. By his account, medicine only serves the public interest to the extent that this is defined by the ruling class. The issue therefore is not whether professional interests are in line with those of the general public, it is whether the 'public interest itself' represents the true needs of the people. Navarro identifies an antagonism between the *real interests of ordinary people* and the stability of the capitalist system. In his view, people would be better off if the system fell apart. He makes the presumption that the collapse of Western capitalism, would usher in a better socialist system and not fascist or totalitarian regimes of the extreme right. But the antagonisms he identifies in capitalist society are so disguised and imprisoned by powerful institutional devices that they do not appear to pose any particular threat to the survival of the system. The inherent contradictions of capitalism, which were the seeds of its downfall for Marx, appear to have been so securely 'packaged' in Navarro's theory, that there is little chance of their seeping out to damage society. This underlines a fundamental difficulty of all 'functionalist' theory. If everything functions together to maintain the stability of the whole, how does change come about? It is ironic that contemporary Marxist interpretations of the *political economy of health* should find themselves so closely allied to the mainstream of conservative American social theory.

This leaves us with Freidson's view of medical power and influence in society. His answer to the question, 'Whose interests does medicine serve?' is quite clear. The profession is primarily devoted to serving its own interests. According to Freidson, doctors have secured such an extraordinary degree of control over the conduct of their work that they are in a class of their own — in short they are socially autonomous. This autonomy has delivered to the profession the unquestioned right to literally define what is health and what is illness, nothing less than a direct participation in the social construction of cultural knowledge. But Freidson is not tempted to elaborate this into a grand theoretical design in which doctors either consciously or unconsciously devote themselves to the preservation of the status quo. His theoretical aims are more modest. He seeks primarily to understand of the role of professions in the labour market and the wider society. His choice of medicine as a case study of professional organisation stems from its contemporary preeminence in the social division of labour. As he notes, among the traditional professions only medicine has developed a systematic connection with science and technology. This has led to the development of a complex division of labour in medical care which is orchestrated and controlled by doctors. Here is further evidence of medical autonomy. The profession not only controls its own conditions of work, it is also in charge of a whole army of helpers ranging from the unskilled to lesser professions.

The source of medical power and autonomy is located by Freidson in political action. It was through collective organisation that the profession was able to successfully negotiate with the state for monopoly rights in the labour market. Esoteric knowledge and technique, are also important and this chapter has argued that there is an ideological dimension to medical power which develops in the aftermath of the profession's successful efforts in the political arena. Freidson's approach emphasises the significance of political and ideological power resources. While he does not deny the existence of capitalist enterprise organised to cash in on medical treatment, he sees no evidence that the character of treatment itself is dictated by it.

It is easier to accept the arguments of Freidson, not least because they are more modest in their scope. Freidson remains sceptical of reductionist explanations, for, as he points out, individual capitalist and socialist countries develop their own highly variable and particular character so that: 'Neither the logic of capitalism nor the logic of socialism can thus get realised in anywhere near a "pure" form.' (Freidson 1977, 486). It is in this spirit that he insists that the autonomy of the medical profession sets its members apart from other workers, bestowing a type of power of much broader social relevance which is quite simply different from economically determined power, or power flowing from an imaginary functional logic of social stability.

Bibliography

Alaszewski, A. and Haywood S. *Crisis in the Health Service* (Croom Helm, London, 1980).

Alderson, M. *International Mortality Statistics* (Macmillan, London, 1981).

Antonovsky, A. 'Conceptual and Methodological Problems in the Study of Resistance Resources and Stressful Life Events' in *Stressful Life Events: Their Nature and Effects* edited by Dohrenwend, B.P. and Dohrenwend, B.S. (John Wiley & Sons, New York, 1974).

Brenner, M.H. *Estimating the Social Cost of national Economic Policy: implications for mental and physical health, and criminal aggression* (Joint Committee of the US Congress, Washington DC, 1976).

Brotherston, J. 'Inequality: Is is Inevitable?' in Carter C.O. and Peel J., eds. (1976).

Brown, G. and Harris, T. *Social Origins of Depression* (Tavistock, London, 1978).

Burnett, M. *Genes, Dreams and Realities* (Medical and Technical Publishing Company Ltd., Aylesbury, Bucks. 1971).

Byrne, P.S. and Long, B.E. *Doctors Talking to Patients* (HMSO, London, 1976).

Carter, C.O. and Peel, J. *Equalities and Inequalities in Health* (Academic Press, London, 1976).

Cartwright, A. and O'Brian, M. 'Social Class, Variations in Health Care and the Nature of General Practitioner Consultations' in *The Sociology of the NHS* edited by M. Stacey (Sociological Review Monograph No. 22, Keele University, 1976).

Cartwright, A. *Patients and their Doctors* (Routledge and Kegan Paul, London, 1967).

Cochrane, A.L. *Effectiveness and Efficiency: Random Reflections on Health Services,* (Nuffield Provincial Hospitals Trust, 1972).

Cooper, R. 'Rising Death Rates in the Soviet Union: The Impact of Coronary Heart Disease' in *New England Journal of Medicine* (Vol. 304: 21: 1259-65, 1981).

Coser, R.L. *Life on the Ward* (University of Illinois Press, East Lansing, 1962).

Davis, C. and Feshbein, M. *Rising Infant Mortality in the USSR in the 1970s* (Government Printing Office, Washington, D.C., Series P.95, No. 74, 1980).

DHSS *Report of the Resource Allocation Working Party* (DHSS, 1976).

DHSS *Inequalities in Health: Report of a Research Working Group* (1981).

Dohrendwend, B.P. and Dohrendwend, B.S. (eds). *Stressful Life Events. Their Nature and Effects* (John Wiley and Sons, New York, 1974).

Doyal, L. and Pennell, I. *The Political Economy of Health* (Pluto Press, London, 1979).

Dubos, R. *Mirage of Health* (Harper & Row, New York, 1959).

Durkheim, E. *The Division of Labour in Society* (The Free Press of Glencoe, Collier-MacMillan Ltd., London, 1964 Ed.)

Durkheim, E. *Suicide* (Routledge and Kegan Paul, London, 1952).

Dutton, J. 'Changes in Soviet Mortality Patterns, 1959-1977' in *Population and Development Review* 5 (pp.267-69, 1977).

Evans-Pritchard, E.E. *The Nuer* (Clarendon Press, Oxford, 1940).

Evans-Pritchard, E.E. *Witchcraft, Oracles and Magic* (Oxford University Press, Oxford, 1978).

Eyer, J. 'Capitalism, Health and Illness' in *Readings in the Political Economy of Health* edited by McKinley J. (pp.23-59) (Tavistock London, 1984).

Ferguson, T. and McPhail, A.N. *Hospital and Community* (Oxford University Press, London, 1954).

Fox, J. *et al Working Paper No. 18,* ESRC *Workshop on Health and Unemployment* (Oct. 26th, 1984).

Freidson, E. *Profession of Medicine* (Dodd, Mead & Co., New York, 1975).

Freidson, E. 'Comment on McKinley' in *International Journal of Health Services* (Vol. 7, No. 3, pp.485-86, 1977).

Friedman, M. and Rosenman, R.H. 'Association of specific overt behaviour pattern with blood and cardiovascular findings'. *Journal of the American Medical Association,* 169, 1286-1296, 1959.

Garfinkel, H. *Studies in Ethnomethodology* (Prentice Hall, Englewood Cliffs, 1967).

Gerhardt, U. 'Coping and Social Action' in *Sociology of Health and Illness* (Vol. 1, No. 2, 1979).

Goffman, E. *Asylums, Essays on the Social Situations of Mental Patients and Other*

134   The Sociology of Health and Medicine

Inmates (Doubleday Anchor, New York, 1961).

Hall, M.H. *et al* 'Is Routine Ante-Natal Care Worthwhile?' *The Lancet* July 1980, 78-80.

Hinkle, L.E. 'The Concept of Stress in the Biological and Social Sciences' in *Science, Medicine and Man* (Vol. 1, 31-48, 1973).

Hinkle L.E. and Wolff H.G. 'The nature of man's adaptation to his total environment and the relation of this to illness' *Archives of Internal Medicine*, No. 22, 1957.

Holmes, T.H. and Rahe, R.H. 'The Social Readjustment Rating Scale' in *The Journal of Psychosomatic Research* (11, 213-18, 1967).

Illich, I. *Medical Nemesis* (Bantam Books, New York, 1977).

Illsley, R. 'Social Class Selection and Class Differences in Relation to Stillbirths' in *The British Medical Journal* (ii, 1520, 1955).

Lazarus, R. *Psychological Stress and the Coping Process* (McGraw Hill, New York, 1966).

Rees, W. and Lutkins, S. 'Mortality and Bereavement' *British Medical Journal* 1967, 4, 13-16.

McKeown, T. *The Modern Rise of Population* (Edward Arnold, London, 1976).

McKeown, T. *The Role of Medicine: Dream, Mirage or Nemesis?* (The Nuffield Provincial Hospitals Trust, London, 1976).

McKinley, J. 'The Business of Good Doctoring or Doctoring as Good Business: Reflections on Freidson's View of the Medical Game' in *International Journal of Health Services* (Vol. 7, No. 3, 459-83, 1977).

McNeill, W., *Plagues and Peoples* (Doubleday, New York, 1976).

Marmott, M.G. *Social Inequalities in Mortality - The Social Environment* (Dept. of Epidemiology, London School of Hygiene, 1982).

Millman, M. *The Unkindest Cut* (Morrow, New York, 1977).

Mishra, R. *Society and Social Policy: Theoretical Perspectives on Welfare* (Macmillan, London 1977).

Navarro, V. *Medicine under Capitalism* (Croom Helm, London, 1976).

OPCS *Longitudinal Study: Socio-demographic mortality differences, 1971-75.* Fox A.J. and Goldblatt P.O. (HMSO, London, 1982)

OPCS *Trends in Mortality* (HMSO, London, 1978).

OPCS *General Household Survey, 1974* (HMSO, London, 1976).

OPCS *Demographic Review, 1977* (HMSO, London, 1978).

OPCS *Occupational Mortality, 1970-72* (HMSO, London, 1978).

Parsons, T. *The Social System* (The Free Press, Glencoe, Illionois, 1951).

Parsons, T. 'The sick role and the role of the physician reconsidered' in *Millbank Memorial Fund Quarterly* (53: 257-78, 1975).

Selye, H. *The Stress of Life* (McGraw Hill, New York, 1956).

Stern, J. *Unemployment and its impact on Morbidity and Mortality* (Discussion Paper No. 93, Centre for Labour Economics, L.S.E.)

Stern, J. 'Social Mobility and the Interpretation of Social Class Mortality Differences' *Journal of Social Policy,* 1981.

Szasz, T. and Hollander, M. 'A contribution to the philosophy of medicine: the basic model of the doctor-patient relationship' in *Archives of Internal Medicine* (97: 585-92, 1956).

Totman, R. *The Social Causes of Illness* (Souvenir Press, London 1979).

Winter, J. 'Aspects of the Impact of the First World War on Infant Mortality in Britain' *Journal of European Economic History* 1982, Vol. 11, 713-738.

Wirth L. 'Urbanism As a Way of Life' *American Sociological Review* 1938, 44, 1-24.

Wrigley, A. and Scofield, R. *The Population History of England 1450-1870* (Cambridge University Press, Cambridge 1981).

Index

138 The Sociology of Health and Medicine

market forces and risk of accidents 43
market, effect on social relationships 26
Marmott, M. 88
married women working 29
Marx, Karl 35-37, 38, 45, 48, 67-68, 100, 110, 131
Marxism 41
Marxist approaches
  to health, parallels with Illich, I. 47
  to medicine 100, 119
  to study of health 38
Marxist theory of class 67
material deprivation as cause of health inequality 62, 64-65
maternal mortality 7, 31
McKeown, T. 4, 6, 12, 25, 31, 32, 33
McKinley, J. 111, 117, 118, 119, 119, 120
McNeill, W. 22, 23
mechanical solidarity 44
medical act of 1858 96, 117
medical care
  and the market place 114
  as citizenship right 113
medical power 110
  and capitalism 111, 117
  ideological bases of 129
medical practice, organisation of 11
medical profession 1, 10, 95, 102, 105, 109
  and control of national resources for health 113
  and the class structure 118
  in Britain 128
  legal privileges of 116
  public confidence in 17
  rise of and industrial capitalism 116
medical technology, impact on health 126
medical theory in the nineteenth century 14
medical treatment
  changing place of 16
  evaluation of 9
  inflation of costs in 123, 126
medicalisation of everyday life 46, 47
medicine achievements of 17
  and capitalism 111
  and control of health policy 10
  and individualism 17
  and process of diagnosis 10
  and religion 17
  and technology 8, 16, 18
  and the profit motive 117
  and the public interest 130
  and the stability of society 129, 130
  as a capitalist commodity 111, 117, 118
  as a social ideology 17, 96, 121, 129
  as a social institution 111, 128
  as institution of social control 110, 129-131

as instrument of class rule 121
as opium of people 49
as secular religion 128
basic research in 13
contribution to contemporary health 9
contribution of to improvements in health 4, 7, 18, 120, 122
effectiveness of 95, 115
evaluation of 116-117, 128
link with capitalism 17, 110
parallels with witchcraft 11, 13
theoretical knowledge of 9, 12, 16
view of disease causation 11
merit awards 124, 126
migration, health risks in 44, 47, 80
Millman, M. 105
mind over matter 78
mind/body dualism 12, 13, 14, 17, 84, 108, 128
Mishra, R. 130
modern rise of population 35
monopoly powers of medicine 95-97, 112, 113, 114, 115, 127, 132
morbidity 3
  limitations of various measures 56
  sex differences in 56
mortality 3, 37
  and population growth 25
mortality, regional inequalities in the UK 62
mortality, sex differences in 4, 28
mortality and morbidity compared 56, 57
mortification of self 105, 106, 107, 128
motivated deviance 97
motherhood 29

National Health Service 1, 3, 8-10, 53, 58, 96, 108, 116, 124-1
  act 1946 124
  and social citizenship 130
  distribution of budget of 127
  regional inequalities in 60
  resource allocation in 60
natural selection
  as cause of health inequality 62, 63, 76
  link with bio-mechanical model 76
Navarro, V. 48, 49, 111, 120, 122, 130, 131
Nuer 78
nursing process 10
nutritional determinism 32

O'Brian, M. 101
OPCS longitudinal survey 54
obstetrics 8
occupational autonomy 112, 118, 119, 122, 123
  as basis of medical power 131, 132
occupational structure, changes in the